YE VIEW
THE
OUNTAINS
MPSHIRE.

COPYRIGHTED BY H.N. TURNER. 1880.

23. Tuckerman's Ravine.	31. Moat Mountain.
24. Carter Dome.	32. Bear Mountain.
25. Spruce Mountain.	33. Lower Gateway of Crawford Notch.
26. Double Head.	34. Upper Gateway of Crawford Notch.
27. Mount Wild-Cat.	
28. Mount Carter.	
30. Mount Kiarsarge.	

HOWE·LIBRARY

HANOVER
NEW HAMPSHIRE

New Hampshire—A Visual History
White Mountains

First NH Banks is proud to have a part in preserving the recorded history of the White Mountains through presentation of this pictorial account of the area's development and progress.

This volume is part of a series produced to preserve the rich heritage of the Granite State. In that regard, we wish to acknowledge and express our sincere appreciation to the authors, the University of New Hampshire, and New Hampshire Public Television for their creative contributions.

Each page of the White Mountains is a salute to the men and women whose untiring efforts created a region rich in cultural, educational, commercial, industrial, and charitable enterprises of which all can be justly proud.

First NH Banks is very much a part of New Hampshire's legacy, and we dedicate this book to all of our citizens—past, present, and future.

① First NH Banks

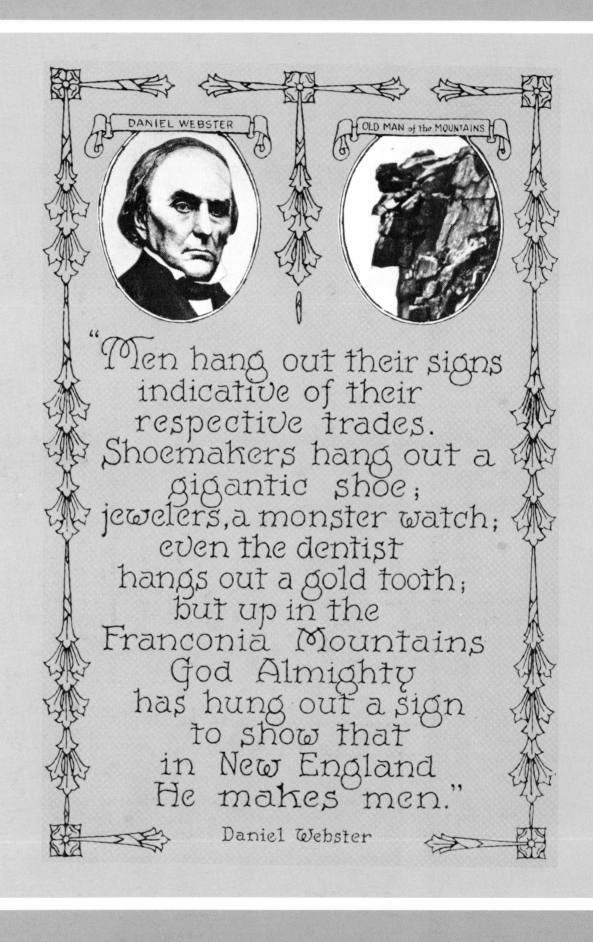

DANIEL WEBSTER

OLD MAN of the MOUNTAINS

"Men hang out their signs
indicative of their
respective trades.
Shoemakers hang out a
gigantic shoe;
jewelers, a monster watch;
even the dentist
hangs out a gold tooth;
but up in the
Franconia Mountains
God Almighty
has hung out a sign
to show that
in New England
He makes men."

Daniel Webster

the WHITE MOUNTAINS

NEW HAMPSHIRE

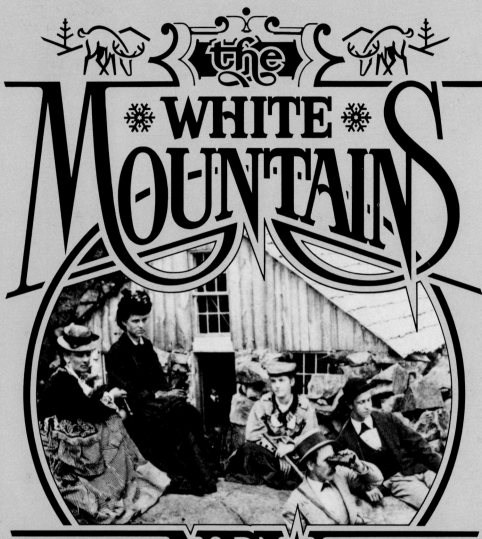

A VISUAL HISTORY

John D. Bardwell & Ronald P. Bergeron

THE
DONNING COMPANY
PUBLISHERS
NORFOLK/VIRGINIA BEACH

To our daughters,
Melissa Bardwell
and
Michelle Bergeron,
for their love and understanding.

The Donning Company/Publishers
5659 Virginia Beach Boulevard
Norfolk, Virginia 23502

Edited by Liliane McCarthy
Richard A. Horwege, Senior Editor

Library of Congress Cataloging-in-Publication Data

Bardwell, John D.
    The White Mountains of New Hampshire.

    Bibliography: p.
    Includes index.
    1. White Mountains (N.H. and Me.)—Description and travel—
Views. 2. White Mountains (N.H. and Me.)—History—Pictorial works.
I. Bergeron, Ronald P. II. Title.
F41.37.B37   1988   974.2'2   88-25822
ISBN 0-89865-737-7 (lim. ed.)

Printed in the United States of America

ACKNOWLEDGMENTS

Many people responded to our request for information, shared their photographs or in some way assisted with the preparation of this volume. We would like to acknowledge the special help of Ellen Chandler, Wildcat Mountain ski area; Dr. Richard Gramly, Buffalo Museum of Science; Richard Ober, Society for the Protection of New Hampshire Forests; James Dolph, Portsmouth Naval Shipyard; Stephen P. Barba, Balsams/Wilderness ski area; Carole L. Wegman, Herbert Schneider and Stephen Rice, Mount Cranmore ski area; Ossipee Historical Society; New Hampshire Historical Society, University of New Hampshire, Dimond Library Special Collections; and Ron White of Ossipee for his original illustrations.

Guy Gosselin, Mount Washington Observatory; Douglas Philbrook, Mount Washington Auto Road; and Charles Bolian, U.N.H. archaeologist, were kind enough to read appropriate sections of the manuscript and apply their special knowledge to a review of the work. They are the true experts of the history of the White Mountains of New Hampshire. We are grateful for their assistance.

CONTENTS

An engraving of Mount Madison and Mount Washington from Shelburne in New Hampshire's White Mountains. Published in Thomas Starr King's The White Hills; Their Legends, Landscape, and Poetry, *circa 1858*

Portrait of Reverend Jeremy Belknap from Volume I of his History of New Hampshire, *which was published in 1831. University of New Hampshire Special Collections*

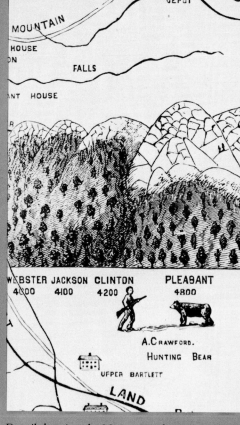

Detail showing the Mount Washington House and the Cog Railway from a Frank Leavitt map of the White Mountains, circa 1878. New Hampshire Historical Society

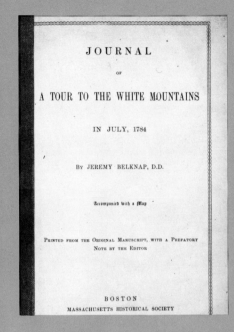

Title page of Jeremy Belknap's Journal of a Tour to the White Mountains in July, 1784. *New Hampshire Historical Society*

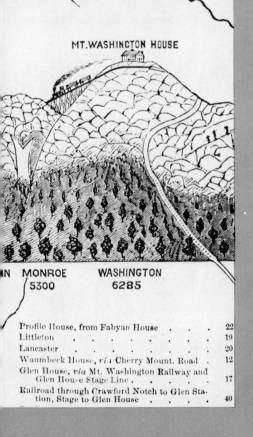

INTRODUCTION

The White Mountain Region covers most of the northern half of New Hampshire and includes the panoramic views and scenic wonders in the White Mountain National Forest. Within this region are eighty-six mountain peaks, nine notches, and the headwaters of the Saco, Androscoggin, Merrimack, and Connecticut rivers. Geologically, the White Mountains belong to the crystalline belt of the Appalachian system and are made up of ancient metamorphic rock with a core of mica schist forming the highest portion. The stern and lofty hills are composed of rocks which have resisted wearing down. This rock gives the treeless summits a whitish-gray appearance when seen from a distance, and the atmospheric conditions make them appear to be white. Snow cover lasts for six months, more or less, so the mountains always look like white clouds rising just above the horizon.

They were described as "the Christal hill," by Christopher Levett in his 1628 publication, *A Voyage into New-England.* Jeremy Belknap's *History of New Hampshire* points out that the explorers of 1642 had great expectation of finding precious stones resembling crystal and they named these mountains the Crystal-hills. Governor Winthrop recorded Darby Field's ascent of Mount Washington in 1642 and described it as "the white hill." He also recorded that "the white hills" were discovered by Field. One Algonquin Indian name, *Agiococbook,* has been translated as "at the mountains on that side." Another Indian name was *Waumbekketmethna.* This translates as "white" *(Waumbekket),* and "mountains" *(methna).* Samuel Drake pointed out that this easily resolves itself into the Kennebec-Abnaki word *waubeghiket-amadinar* which translates to "white greatest mountain."

The name *White Mountains* is sometimes applied to a group of hills that includes the New Hampshire ranges and peaks and the adjacent hills in western Maine. The range containing the highest peaks has been designated the Presidential Range because most of the mountains have been named after presidents of the United States.

Mount Washington is the summit of the White Mountains of New Hampshire. It rises 4,000 feet above its bases at the east and west and is 6,288 feet above sea level. The Presidential Range was formed 260 million years ago, and Mount Washington is one of the world's oldest mountains. Fifty thousand years ago it was covered by the Wisconsin ice cap, and pebbles brought by the ice from Jefferson, New Hampshire, have been found on the top of Mount Washington.

Above the timber line, there is nothing but broken masses of rock, clumps of sparse grasses, lichens, dwarf furs, and stunted spruce as far as the eye can see. The soil, vegetation, animal life, and insect life are like those of the subarctic. From sun to shadow, temperatures can vary as much as fifty degrees.

The White Mountains have attracted explorers, settlers, loggers, vacationers, hikers, and skiers for over three hundred years. When Phineas Barnum saw the view from the observation tower on Mount Washington, he was reputed to have called it "the second greatest show on earth!"

1
INDIANS AND EXPLORERS

The tribes inhabiting the foothills and river valleys of the White Mountains belonged to the Abnaki group of the great Algonquin family. This included the Sokokis on the Saco and the Arosagunticooks, or Anasagunticooks, on the Androscoggin. The Sokokis were divided into numerous branches, of which the Ossipees and the Pequawkets were the most prominent.

These Indians relied on hunting, fishing and food gathering for their subsistence. Their agriculture was very limited, although Belknap reported that their fields were visible in many places. There was evidence of the destruction of trees by girdling. Their campsites are usually discovered on the banks of rivers, near ponds, or on the shores of lakes.

Passaconaway was a great chief of the Pennacook Confederation. He was a physical and intellectual giant who had forged an alliance with over a dozen tribes to resist the attacks of the dreaded Mohawks. At one time Passaconaway governed over three thousand people, and he could muster an army of over five hundred experienced fighting men. However, shortly before the arrival of the Pilgrims, a pestilence swept through the Indian villages of New England. It was so severe that some powerful tribes were reduced to a handful of forlorn survivors.

A PREHISTORIC WORKSHOP AT MOUNT JASPER

Mount Jasper, located within the city limits of Berlin, New Hampshire, has a rhyolite of superior flaking qualities which outcrops near the highest point of the hill. An ancient quarry, dug ten meters into the rock, provided significant evidence of primitive industry. Well-developed joints in the rhyolite enabled the miners to extract chunks of rock using hammerstones, perhaps wooden wedges, and other perishable materials.

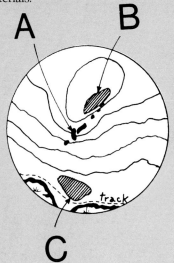

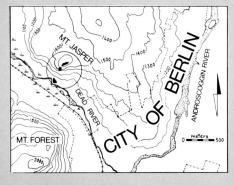

A topographic map of Mt. Jasper and vicinity. The location of the ancient mine (A) is shown at the edge of a plateau upland. The shaded aras of the map insert are workshops (B, C) located above and below excavated rhyolite outcrops (darkened areas). Richard M. Gramly

The Mount Jasper workshop is located at the base of the mountain just above the Dead River, a tributary of the Androscoggin. Level areas on the rocky promontory were used as work sites by the early stone knappers, and dense concentrations of flaking debris accumulated. The lack of postholes and hearths probably indicates that the pre-historic stone knappers remained only long enough to replenish their tool kits. The short growing season and harsh climate did not make this an ideal site for permanent occupation.

View of the eastern face of Mt. Jasper from the grounds of the Berlin public school. Arrow indicates the area of prehistoric quarrying. Richard M. Gramly

Entrance to the prehistoric rhyolite mine. The archaeologist is standing on a floor of soil fill and quarry debris. The rhyolite pillar that was left to support the roof of the mine can be seen in the extreme upper right of the picture. Richard M. Gramly

Sketch of prehistoric mine at Mt. Jasper. Note the pillar that was left to support the roof of the mine. Dimensions are approximate. Richard M. Gramly

Workshop areas were excavated on the top of Mount Jasper near the site of an ancient trench in the rhyolite dike and at the base of the mountain on the banks of the Dead River. Concentrations of flakes in these workshops suggest that the miners of the archaic period processed less rhyolite than those of a later period. They probably lacked canoes, traveled on foot, and made brief stops on periodic trips through the region. The recovery of significant numbers of reworked tools, especially projectile points which exhibited old breakage, is evidence that this was a site where hunters stopped, and not a site where projectile points were being produced as trade items. The reworked projectile points have been dated within the last few centuries before European settlement and resemble tools from the Maine coast and the maritimes. This would suggest that the Saint John River, rather than the Androscoggin, may have been the route to the coast for hunters from the interior.

View of the archaeological excavations in progress along the Dead River below Mt. Jasper. Many thousands of flakes and rejected stone tools were unearthed at this site. Richard M. Gramly

Specimens excavated from the ancient workshop along the bank of the Dead River immediately below Mt. Jasper. They illustrate the evolution of a bifacial preform to a corner-notched projectile point. Richard M. Gramly

In some cases, there were not enough left to bury the dead. Sir Richard Hawkins visited the coast in 1615 and reported seeing unburied skeletons bleaching in deserted wigwams. Passaconaway was reported being present at Plymouth in 1620, when the Pilgrims arrived on the *Mayflower*. He became known to the white men in 1623, when Captain Levett reported to have seen him. In 1629 he granted a large tract of land between the Piscataqua and the Merrimac rivers to the Reverend John Wheelright and other members of the Massachusetts Bay Colony. John Eliot's preaching so impressed the Indians that he was invited to live with them as their teacher. Passaconaway was probably converted at this time.

In 1660 Passaconaway was succeeded by his son Wonalancet, who had been converted to Christianity by John Eliot. When he could no longer restrain his warriors from attacking the colonists, he gave up the chieftaincy and moved to St. Francis in Canada. Kancamagus, a nephew, became chief in 1685. He made several attempts to remain friends with the colonists but was badly treated. In 1689 he led the terrible attack on Dover. After the truce of Sagadahoc, Kancamagus disappeared, probably to St. Francis.

The easternmost peak of the Sandwich Range was known and mapped as Conway Peak, decades before it was named for the legendary Indian Chocorua. According to the stories, Chocorua refused to retreat to Canada when the Pequawket Indians were defeated after Lovewell's battle in 1725. He became friendly with the incoming white settlers and left his son with one of them while he was away on a long journey. The son was accidentally poisoned and Chocorua apparently took his vengeance on the man's wife and children. The man tracked Chocorua to the crest of the mountain and shot him down. (Another version of the legend describes Chocorua jumping to his death.) The dying Indian cursed white men and the Chocorua legend has been the subject of a number of poems including a juvenile production by Longfellow. One version of the curse is as follows:

> A curse upon ye, white men! May the Great Spirit curse ye when he speaks in the clouds, and his words are fire! Chocorua had a son, and ye killed him while the sky looked bright! Lightning blast your crops! The Evil Spirit breathe death on your cattle! Your graves lie in the warpath of the Indian! Panthers howl and wolves fatten upon your bones! Chocorua goes to the Great Spirit—but his curse stays with the white men!

The Indians who inhabited the White Mountain region lived in awe of the highest peaks, usually cloud-capped and snow-covered for many months, and the source of rock slides and thunderstorms. It has been said that they considered the ascent of these peaks to be both perilous and sacrilegious. The most intriguing of the Indian legends was that of the Great Carbuncle, a huge gem that gave off a brilliant light. This gem was supposed to have been placed under a rock shelf by the Indians

A late 1800s view of Mount Kearsarge from the Saco River in North Conway, New Hampshire. New Hampshire Historical Society

who killed one of their companions so that an evil spirit would haunt the place and prevent people from disturbing the carbuncle. The legend was immortalized by Nathaniel Hawthorne in his *Twice-told Tales*.

It is impossible to say which of the European explorers first discovered the White Mountains, since they can be seen from the sea on a clear day. The Florentine navigator Verrazano first reported seeing them in 1524. He was sailing along the coast of New England near Portsmouth and wrote that he saw "high mountains within the land." The French explorer Samuel de Champlain was sailing in the vicinity of Portland in 1605 when he wrote in his journal, "From here large mountains are seen to the west." The Englishman Christopher Levett, in the account of his voyage to New England in 1623 and 1624, reported: "This river (the Saco), as I am told by the Salvages [*sic*], commeth from a great mountain called Christall hill, being as they say 100 miles in the Country."

Darby Field is generally credited with being the first European to visit the mountains. In 1642 he climbed to

Indians of the White Mountains.
Illustration by Ron White

the top of Mount Washington with the assistance of Indian guides. While on the "Christall hill" he gathered shining stones which he mistook for diamonds. His reports of shining stones led to the other expeditions into the mountains including one sponsored by Sir Ferdinando Gorges, the proprietor of the Province of Maine.

In his 1674 *Account of Two Voyages to New England*, John Josselyn described the country as "Rockie and Mountanious, full of tall wood. One stately mountain there is surmounting the rest, about four score mile from the Sea. The black flies are so numerous...that a man cannot draw his breath, but he will suck them in." He speculated that the mountains were first raised by earthquakes and that one could determine that they were hollow by the sound of the rain on the level areas at the top.

The French and their Indian allies fought bitterly to

slow the English settlement in northern New England. As the English pushed northward and westward, the White Mountains took on new importance. Several Massachusetts and New Hampshire militia units marched to the region. In 1725 one of these units was defeated at Lovewell Pond and a ranging party climbed to the top of Mount Washington. King George's War (1743-1748) and the French and Indian War (1755-1763) prevented the hardy Scotch-Irish immigrants from moving into the White Mountains. The pass called Crawford Notch was known to the Indians, and war parties from Canada used the route in making raids on the New England coast. They also used the route when they were returning to Canada with their captives.

The Indian stronghold at St. Francis, near Quebec, was destroyed by Major Robert Rogers and his rangers, who made a three-week trek through the wilderness,

A DISCOVERY OF THE NOTCH

Crawford Notch was discovered by two hunters, Nash and Sawyer, when they followed a moose along a mountain stream surrounded by towering rock walls. They eventually learned that they were on an ancient Indian trail which opened into a meadow on the other side of the mountains. The hunters published this interesting discovery. Their reward was a tract of land north of the notch which was appropriately known as "Nash and Sawyer's Location."

The entrance to the notch was a natural gateway about twenty-two feet wide. The Saco River rises from a little beaver meadow to the north, passes through the narrow passage, and runs south to the ocean.

The first settler through the notch was Colonel Whipple of Portsmouth, who struggled through the mountains with his cattle and settled in Dartmouth, now Jefferson. Whipple came in 1772 and his servant, Granny Stalbird, in 1776,

became the first woman through the notch. She learned the medicinal value of roots and herbs from the Indians and became famous for her skills as a healer.

The Willey House was the oldest house erected in the notch. It was built in 1793 by Mr. Davis to accommodate travelers. It was later purchased and expanded by the Willey family who perished in the avalanche of 1826.

Early photograph of the road through Crawford Notch. It follows the Saco River which starts in a little beaver meadow and runs south, through the notch, to the ocean. Ossipee Historical Society

From a stereoview by N. W. Pease called "Summer Rambles in North Conway." U.N.H. Special Collections

Crawford Notch and the Willey House from an 1848 lithograph by Isaac Sprague for William Oakes' Scenery of the White Mountains.

Passaconaway, chief of the Pennacook Confederation, who governed over three thousand people until disease swept through the villages and killed many of his followers. New Hampshire Historical Society

slaughtered most of the Indians, burned the village, shot the priest, and stole the silver and gold service from the church. Only a handful of the rangers survived the return trip, but they succeeded in eliminating the threat of attack from St. Francis. In 1746 Governor Benning Wentworth purchased the rights of John Mason from his heirs and deeded the land back to inhabitants in all the settled towns. Once the Indians were driven north, settlers began to move up from the coast. In 1764 the governor granted twenty-three thousand acres on the eastern slopes at Conway. Among the first settlers were Elijah Dinsmore and his wife, who hiked eighty miles, carrying their possessions on their backs, and sleeping each night on the snow.

Grants were authorized for the townships of Gilmanton, Meredith, Sanbornton, Tuftonboro, Wakefield, and Holderness by 1750. There was continued interest in the North Country, even though these settlements were developing very slowly. The provincial government of New Hampshire made plans to survey the upper reaches of the Connecticut River and build a road into the region.

The conquest of French Canada by the English and Americans in 1760 made the frontier safe for settlement. Governor Benning Wentworth granted townships on both sides of the Connecticut. The land to the west of the river, known as the New Hampshire Grants, was recognized as the state of Vermont in 1791. Exploration and settlement continued at a steady pace during the revolutionary period. Settlement stimulated exploration and each new discovery led to new settlements.

Two views of Mount Chocorua taken approximately one hundred years apart. The glass negative was exposed circa 1890 (Ossipee Historical Society) and the more recent photograph was taken by Gary Samson in 1987.

An engraving of Indian chief Chocorua, a Pequawket whose tragic attempt to live among the white settlers cost him his life. The easternmost peak of the Sandwich Range is now named after this legendary Indian. New Hampshire Historical Society

A portrait of Governor Benning Wentworth. His landgrants encouraged settlers to move up from the coast and establish new townships in the North Country.

An early nineteenth-century engraving
of a view near Conway, New Hampshire,
by Fenner, Sears & Company, after a
painting by Thomas Cole. Courtesy of
New Hampshire Historical Society

2
THE PERIOD OF SETTLEMENT

The more remote regions of New Hampshire could not be settled until the latter part of the eighteenth century, when the country was fairly safe from Indian depredations. Nathaniel Smith built a cabin on the site of the ancient Indian village of Pequawket and moved his family to the grant in the summer of 1763. To reach their new home, they had to travel through nearly seventy miles of unbroken wilderness. The only mode of transportation was horses, and the only road was a blazed trail. Their nearest white neighbors and their source of supplies were in Sanford or Saco. It was on this site, in 1725, that Capt. John Lovewell and thirty-four men had engaged the Indians in a furious battle. Thirteen of Lovewell's men had been left dead or dying, four others had been left behind on the trail, and there had been only eleven in the party when it returned. The Indians abandoned the village and moved to St. Francis on the St. Lawrence River.

One of the first places to be settled in the White Hills was Conway. The site was granted to Daniel Foster by Gov. Benning Wentworth in 1756. The grant covered

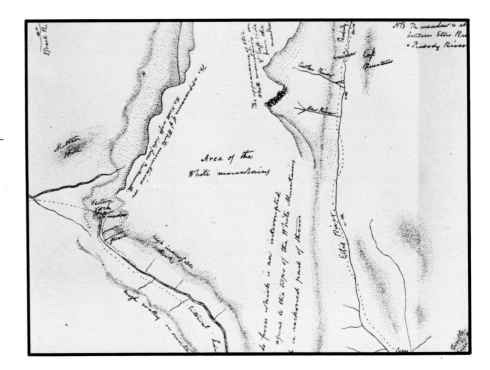

Section of a map drawn by Jeremy Belknap in his 1784 journal, Tour to the White Mountains. *Courtesy of New Hampshire Historical Society*

White Horse Ledge as it appeared in the 1890s. Courtesy of Ossipee Historical Society

23,040 acres of land with another 1,040 acres for roads, ponds, and mountains. Glowing accounts of the fertility of the soil and the abundance of game attracted settlers from Concord, Pembroke, Exeter, Portsmouth, Durham, and Lee. Foster led several other settlers five miles north, where they built homes and established the settlement of North Conway.

The town of Jefferson was settled about 1773 by Col. Joseph Whipple, the first settler through Crawford Notch. He owned a vast area and had great influence over those who chose to settle in the vicinity. This is the same site where detachments of Roger's Rangers were captured or killed by Indians after they destroyed the Indian Village at St. Francis. The white men carried off the church plate, candlesticks, and a large silver image. The golden candlesticks of the church of St. Francis were found near Lake Memphremagog in 1816, but the silver image has never been recovered.

Granny Stalbird, or Starbird, was thought to be the first woman to come through the notch. A servant of Colonel Whipple, she learned the medicinal value of roots and herbs from the Indians. In her later years she provided medical care for the people in the region.

Lancaster was settled in 1763 by Capt. David Page, Edward Bucknam, Emmons Stockwell, and their families. Tensions caused by the Revolutionary War caused all but

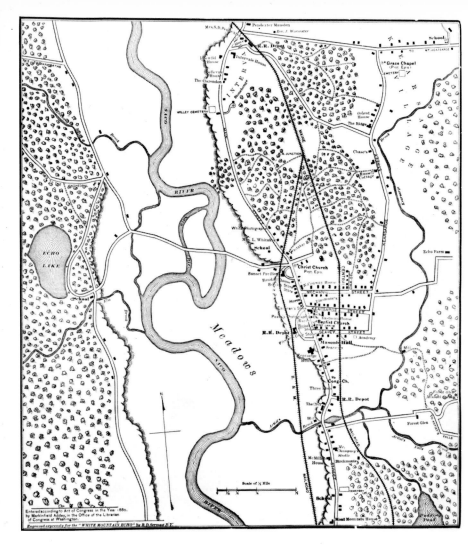

Map from The White Mountain Echo *showing Conway in 1883-84. Courtesy of University of New Hampshire Special Collections*

A Kilburn Brothers' photograph of a farm scene in Jefferson, New Hampshire, circa 1880. Courtesy of New Hampshire Historical Society

Stockwell to move to more established communities. Stockwell's determination to stay in his new home convinced some of the others to return, and the Lancaster settlement survived.

Littleton was chartered in 1764 under the name of Chiswick. It was rechartered in 1770 as Apthorp and first settled by Capt. Moses Caswell. The name was changed to Littleton in 1784.

Franconia was granted in 1764, but was permanently settled in 1774, when Capt. Artemas Knight, Zebedee Applebee, and others arrived and became involved in a dispute with the original grantees. They renamed the area Morristown, but the name Franconia was restored in 1782, when the dispute was settled. The town owed its early prosperity to the discovery of iron ore. The New Hampshire Iron Factory Company was incorporated in 1805 and the ironworks were located on the Gale River. A blast furnace, cupola furnace, forge, and machine shop employed twenty to thirty men and produced approximately two hundred and fifty tons of pig iron and up to three hundred tons of bar iron annually. The rich ore was mined from a mountain in Lisbon, which was three miles from the furnace. Not far from this plant was the Haverhill and Franconia Iron Works, which was incorporated in 1808.

Jackson was settled by Benjamin Copp and his family

Nancy's Brook and Nancy's Bridge were named after a servant girl who was employed by Colonel Whipple, the first settler in Jefferson. Nancy was engaged to a man who also worked for Colonel Whipple, and they planned to accompany the colonel on his fall visit to Portsmouth, where they would be married. A few days before their departure she was tricked into giving her savings to her lover for safekeeping before she left on a nine-mile trip to Lancaster to purchase items needed for the long journey to Portsmouth.

While Nancy was in Lancaster, the Colonel and her lover left for Portsmouth without her. She learned of their departure and returned to Jefferson determined to follow them. She left at night, in a blinding snowstorm, the path hidden by deep snow. Her objective was to reach Colonel Whipple's camp in the notch, which was thirty miles away. Nancy reached the camp only to find that they had already left. She tried to follow but fell in the stream, since called Nancy's Brook. She was found on the opposite bank, at the foot of an aged tree, her head resting upon her staff, frozen to death. Her treacherous lover died a few years later, a raving maniac, in a madhouse.

Nancy's Bridge, *a lithograph by Isaac Sprague, was produced in 1848 for William Oakes'* Scenery of the White Mountains.

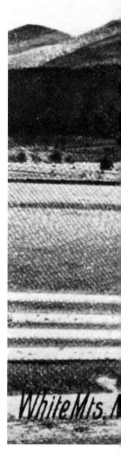

The Presidential Range from the Highland Road in Jefferson. A post card view. From the author's collection

in 1778. They were the only settlers until Capt. Joseph Pinkham, after whom Pinkham Notch is named, came with his family in 1790. It was reported that the snow was five feet deep on the level when they arrived and they used a hand sled drawn by a pig that had been trained to work in harness. The settlement was first called New Madbury and later Adams. In 1829 the name was changed to Jackson.

Berlin was granted to Sir Edward Mayne, several members of his family, and others from Barbados in 1771. The original name was Maynesborough, but it was changed to Berlin when the town was incorporated in 1829. Bartlett, incorporated in 1790, was originally granted to William Stark and others for services in the French and Indians War. In 1777 Daniel Fox, Paul Jilly, and Capt. Samuel Willey established themselves in the area of Upper Bartlett. Whitefield was granted as Whitefields, to Josiah Moody, in 1774. It was settled soon after by Major

Burns and others.

Bethlehem is on the sight of the lost town of "Lord's Hill" or "Lloyd Hills," which was granted by Governor Wentworth around 1774. The first settlement was made by Jonas Warren in 1790, and it was incorporated as Bethlehem in 1799. The early inhabitants suffered great privations and were frequently on the verge of famine. They lived in log huts and tried to raise crops in the rough and rocky soil. On one occasion, they had to survive on roots and plants until their representatives could return from Concord, Massachusetts, with provisions that had been exchanged for a load of potash.

Lisbon was first granted to Joseph Burt under the name of Concord. It apparently included much of the same territory included in the Chiswick grant. Neither town was settled and another charter was issued to Leonard Whiting in 1768. It was called Gunthwaite until 1824, when the legislature changed the name to

Jefferson, Presidential Range from the Highland Road.

Lisbon. Gold was discovered in 1886 and many mining operations were established. Large sums of money were invested by prospectors, but most of the investors were unsuccessful.

Woodstock has vague records of its early history but some local historians believe that the town was first settled by John Riant and others in 1773. According to this theory, the town, originally granted under the name of Peeling, was called Fairfield for a period of time, then was again called Peeling until 1840, when it was changed to Woodstock. Other historians believe that it was granted under the name of Fairfield and that the town charter of 1799 changed the name to Peeling. These claim that the first settler was James McNorton, who died at Valley Forge, leaving a wife and family alone in the wilderness.

Randolph was called Durand until 1824. The first settlers were Joseph Wilder and Stephen Jillson. Carroll was called Bretton Woods until it was incorporated in

1832. Warren was granted to John Page and others in 1763. Settlement was begun by Joseph Patch who lived alone in the area abandoned by the Pemigewassets when they retired to Canada. The area had been the scene of much conflict and continued to be a route for bands of Indians from Canada who were sent to attack the Massachusetts settlements. John Mills brought his family in the spring of 1768 and he was followed by James Aiken, Joshua Copp, and a Mr. True.

Gorham was chartered in 1769, granted as Shelburne Addition in 1770, and settled shortly after that date. It was incorporated as Gorham in 1836. Campton and Rumney were established by a grant made in 1761. Thornton was granted in 1763 and settled by Benjamin Hoit in 1770. Sandwich was granted to Samuel Gilman, Jr., and others of Exeter in 1763. The grantees reported that the north and west sides of the grant were uninhabitable mountains and rocks, so Governor Wentworth provided an additional

Haymaking in Franconia Notch in the late 1800s. The photo was made by the Kilburn Brothers of Littleton, who photographed thousands of White Mountain scenes during this period. Courtesy of New Hampshire Historical Society

INDIAN STREAM REPUBLIC

Pittsburg is the northernmost town in New Hampshire. The area was unexplored until 1787 and was a favorite hunting grounds for the Indians of St. Francis. Two of Roger's Rangers did some hunting and trapping in the area and encouraged others to return with them the next year. It was originally known as Indian Stream Territory and was claimed by both Canada and the state of New Hampshire. The Indians deeded the land to the settlers in 1796, and in 1829 the inhabitants set up an independent state known as the "United Inhabitants of the Indian Stream Territory."

The republic continued to be independent for about five years while Canada and New Hampshire battled for control. The Canadians sent an armed force to capture a deputy sheriff, but the settlers armed themselves and recaptured the deputy in a sharp battle. In 1840 Indian Stream Territory became part of New Hampshire and its name was changed to Pittsburg. The area was definitely awarded to New Hampshire by the terms of the Webster-Ashburton Treaty, signed in 1842.

A post card view of Pittsburg, New Hampshire. Courtesy of Stephen P. Barba

A post card showing Franconia Notch as seen from Sugar Hill. From the author's collection

Profile Rock is more than twelve hundred feet above the level of the road. It is composed of three separate masses of rock, one of which forms the forehead, the second the nose and upper lip, and the third the chin. There is one location on the road leading through the notch where the profile stands out in bold relief against the sky. As one passes down the road, the Old Man's countenance changes into a toothless old woman in a mob cap. Eventually the nose and face flatten until the forehead alone is seen.

The length of the profile from the top of the forehead to the point of the chin is eighty feet. The face looks toward the south-east and is approximately a half-mile from the observer in the road.

At the base of the mountain is a quiet little pond about a quarter of a mile in length, and half as wide, appropriately called Profile Lake. There have been reports that it was never frequented by Indians from fear of the stern image reflected in it.

Colonel C. H. Greenleaf, who began a long stay at the Profile House in 1857, made many visits to the head of the Old Man. From the beginning he noticed that the large stone which forms the foremost part of the forehead had moved forward from the parent rock. Many years later, when he was manager of the firm of Taft & Greenleaf, owners of the Profile and Flume hotels, he became concerned about a Boston newspaper article warning that the face was in danger of falling into the valley. There were many suggestions on how to preserve the Old Man's head, but nothing was done until 1915, when Reverend Guy Roberts from Whitefield took expert stone mason Edward H. Geddes to examine the rock.

Geddes suggested a system of turn-buckles and lewises that would fasten one end of a hinge to solid rock and the other end to a loose stone. The loose stone could be lifted several inches by ice, but it would always come back into place again. The popular landmark was located on the property of the Profile and Flume Hotels Company. Colonel Greenleaf was president of that company and he discussed the proposal with Governor Spaulding who agreed to share in the expense of the under-taking. Geddes was engaged to do the

The classic profile of the "Old Man of the Mountains" a photographed by B. W. Kilburn and sold as a stereograph, circa 1880. From the author's collection

work.

The tools and turnbuckles had to be carried up the mountain and eleven-inch holes had to be drilled in the stone. Work began on September 25. Heavy rain, wind, ice, and cold temperatures made the work very difficult. It took eight days to install the turnbuckles. Geddes worked twelve or more hours each day with very little help. Each of the turnbuckles was designed to hold seventy tons, and the stones that they held weighed only about twenty-five tons. Greenleaf, Geddes, and Roberts were then satisfied that they had done everything possible to preserve the image of the Old Man of the Mountain.

Five miles south of Franconia Notch, in the town of Lincoln, the Pemigewasset River has worn a cavity, known as the Basin, in the solid rock. It is forty feet in diameter and twenty-eight feet deep. Over the years, the rushing water has whirled rocks around in its current so that the solid rock has been worn to its present shape and depth. It is almost perfectly circular, and the water swirls around several times with great velocity until it escapes on the opposite side. The water is ten or twelve feet deep and the sides of the basin are very smooth and regular.

The Basin is a cavity, forty feet in diameter, that has been worn into solid rock by the rushing water of the Pemigewasset River. This photograph was taken by B. W. Kilburn of Littleton, New Hampshire. From the author's collection

grant called the Sandwich Addition. Early settlers were Daniel Beede, John Prescott, David Bean, Jeremiah Page, and Richard Sinclair.

Tamworth was granted to John Webster, Jonathan Moulton, and others, in 1766. It was settled five years later by Richard Jackman, Jonathan Choate, David Philbrick, and William Eastman. These pioneer settlers suffered from a lack of supplies during the first winter and their families nearly starved. They were forced to travel thirty to forty miles for grain and had to kill deer and other wild animals in order to avoid starvation. Near the town is a small settlement that was long called Tamworth Iron Works. An iron factory was built there to process bog iron ore from Ossipee Lake. It produced nails, tools, and anchors for the shipbuilders of Portsmouth. These products were hauled to the coast on sledges. Tamworth Iron Works is now called Chocorua.

The settlers of the White Mountain Region moved slowly and quietly into the uninhabited forests. They went up the rivers in canoes and led oxcarts filled with meager belongings and precious tools. Every member of the

family worked from dawn to dusk to clear farmland, remove stumps, plow the stump-filled rocky fields, and plant wheat and corn. They cut firewood, made maple sugar, gathered berries and nuts, trapped for furs, and hunted for food. They were constantly threatened by wolves, bears, and other wild animals that would attempt to kill their farm animals. Poor crops, marauding Indians, severe storms, and medical problems were a severe test to their endurance. Hundreds of small farms were started after the Revolutionary War but most were abandoned and reclaimed by the forest. Many absentee proprietors created towns with little regard for the topography. They assigned lots on a grid pattern that spread settlers over a wide area and failed to create a centralized village. Even successful farmers found themselves far from the markets with no rivers or roads nearby on which to move their products. In order to survive, North Country farmers had to raise a wide variety of crops and animals, hunt and trap in the fall, cut lumber in the winter, and produce maple sugar in the spring.

By the 1830s, population growth had slowed. Many

Many natural profiles have been sculptured in the rock cliffs of the White Mountains. The Washington profile was recorded in Thorn Mountain Park, Jackson, New Hampshire. From the author's collection

This scenic view of Jackson, New Hampshire, was taken at the turn of the century. Courtesy of New Hampshire Historical Society

From a stereograph of Goodrich Falls, Bartlett, New Hampshire. From the author's collection

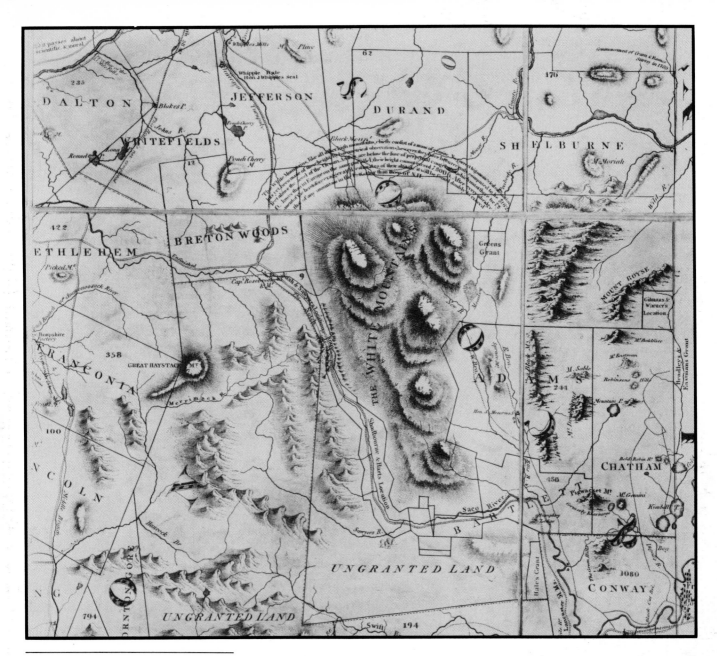

Detail of Phillip Carrigan's 1816 map of the White Mountains. Courtesy of New Hampshire Historical Society

towns experienced a reduction in population and several were actually abandoned. In those towns that experienced growth, expansion tended to come from within. The population moved toward the village centers. Abandoned farms were reclaimed by the forest and purchased by land speculators and lumber companies.

Giant's Grave was a large mound facing Mount Washington, north of Crawford Notch. It was here that young Abel Crawford built a bark-roofed cabin. He hunted and trapped throughout the region while living alone in his tiny cabin. In 1792 Capt. Eleazar Rosebrook and his family moved into the area and Abel married one of his daughters. When their family outgrew the little hut, he moved down through the notch to the present site of

Bemis. As the traffic in the notch increased, Abel helped Rosebrook build a two-story frame house at Giant's Grave, where they could provide shelter for teamsters.

Abel Crawford and his wife raised three daughters and eight huge sons. The oldest was Ethan Allen, who grew up to be the first great trail builder and mountain guide. He enlisted in the War of 1812, but returned when he learned that his grandfather Rosebrook was dying of cancer. Ethan came back to take over the debts, inn, and farm.

He married his cousin Lucy, enlarged the inn to accommodate the increase in teamsters and visitors, blazed the renowned Crawford path, and guided many famous visitors to the summit of Mount Washington. In

CHOCORUA PEAK HOUSE

Jim Liberty of Tamworth built a road and a path on Mount Chocorua which originated at the Charles Durrell house in Tamworth and went three and three-fourths miles to an old logging camp in Albany. The road ended at a halfway house and stable, and an improved path led to the peak. Near the top of the mountain, just under the cone, he built a camp with split stone walls and a canvas roof. The canvas roof blew off and material for a wooden roof burned in a sawmill fire, so he pitched two tents inside the rock walls. Liberty set up a stove outside the walls and was ready for business. If the tents were filled, he slept outside next to the stove.

In 1891 David Knowles of Silver Lake bought the Chocorua Mountain Road and halfway house from Jim Liberty and built the three-story Peak House to replace Jim's primitive lodge. Building the large house on the mountain was a tremendous challenge. Everything had to be brought up from the base by horseback, oxen, or manpower. Four horses were required to bring the stove up the mountain. Knowles even hauled up an organ and put it in the parlor for entertaining.

The first floor had a kitchen, dining room, parlor, and small room some-times referred to as the "bridal suite." There were several bedrooms on the second floor and a dormitory on the third floor. Mr. and Mrs. Knowles operated the Peak House as a summer hotel for many years. In 1914 Mrs. Emma Nickerson became the cook and housekeeper. David Knowles had a horse named Gypsy who was an accomplished mountain climber. Gypsy would go down the mountain, unaccompanied, and walk to Gilman Brothers Store at Silver Lake. Knowles strung a telephone line between the Peak House and Gilman's store. He would phone in his grocery order while Gypsy was wandering down the mountain. The Gilmans would pack the order, attach it to the horse's back, give the animal a slap on the flank, and Gypsy would wander back up the mountain with the groceries.

On September 26, 1915, the Peak House was blown off the mountain in a severe wind storm. The hotel was not open in 1915, but the Knowles family and friends used it occasionally that year. Fortunately, they did not use it after Labor Day, and there was no one in the building when it was completely destroyed by the storm.

The Peak House on Mount Chocorua.
Courtesy of Ossipee Historical Society

A Bethlehem, New Hampshire, farm-house nestled at the base of Mount Agassiz, in the late 1800s. Courtesy of New Hampshire Historical Society

This view of Mount Moriah in Gorham, New Hampshire, was engraved for publication in Thomas Starr King's The White Hills: Their Legends, Landscape, and Poetry, *circa 1858.*

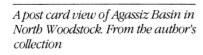

A post card view of Agassiz Basin in North Woodstock. From the author's collection

Boiling down maple sap in the late 1800s. Courtesy of New Hampshire Historical Society

1821, seeking an easier and shorter route, Ethan and his men cleared a trail from his inn to the base and from there up the Ammonoosuc near the line presently used by the cog railway. Two shelters were constructed near the base camp, one for men and one for women. He built more additions to his inn as the number of travelers increased.

In the summers he fished with his visitors, and he hunted in the fall. He brought several bear cubs home for the entertainment of his guests. He also brought home wolf pups, kept a lovely fawn, a peacock, and a guinea hen.

Abel Crawford had a small inn at the southern end of Crawford Notch, but there was need for shelter on the twelve-mile stretch between the two facilities. Samuel Willey came up from Bartlett with his wife and five children to occupy a small abandoned house that would serve stormbound travelers. They enlarged the house and barn to provide the space required for teams and teamsters. In August 1826, a deluge of rain started avalanches on the slopes, and the Willeys decided to move their children to a rock shelter near the mountain base. As they left the house, a tremendous mass of earth, rock, and shattered trees started sliding straight for their home. The mass was split by a granite ledge and passed on either side of the house. However, it caught the entire Willey family, buried some, and swept the others into the Saco River. Every member of the Willey family perished in the slide.

Trappers pose with their dogs in front of a camp deep in the New Hampshire wilderness. Courtesy of New Hampshire Historical Society

Storm on Mount Willey, an 1882 illustration by W. H. Gibson for S. A. Drake's book Heart of the White Mountains.

FIRST HORSE UP THE MOUNTAIN

Abel Crawford was the first man to ride a horse up the rocks of Mount Washington, in 1840. The old man was seventy-five years old at the time and his flowing locks were white. Holding the horse by the reins was his son, Tom Crawford. The path carried visitors as far as the scrub vegetation extended, but it was still a rocky climb to the summit. The availability of the bridle path attracted more visitors to the region.

This portrait of Abel Crawford was painted by Chester Harding in 1846.

ROAD BUILDING

Ethan Allen Crawford spent the winter of 1827 buying and laying in a larger share of provisions than usual, to assist weary travelers braving rough roads in deep snows and feeding those who would require provisions while working to improve the road.

In the spring he went to work on his mountain road as soon as the ground would permit. He made a road, suitable for a carriage, that extended one-and-a-half miles into the woods. It was then possible to ride in a carriage three miles from his house to the end of the road. Passengers would try their strength up the mountain and back where the coach would be waiting to bring them home again. His intention was to work on the road every year until the coaches could run to the foot of Mount Washington.

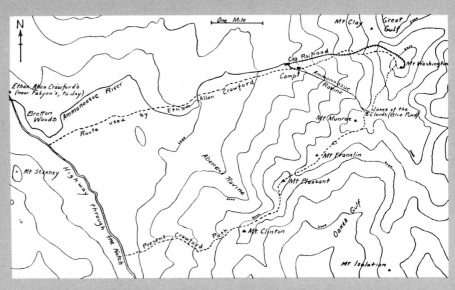

Map of Ethan Allen Crawford's bridle path from near Fabyan to the summit of Mount Washington.

Mount Washington and the White Hills from near Crawfords, *from an engraving after W. H. Bartlett. Courtesy of New Hampshire Historical Society*

An early road to Mount Washington, circa 1890. Courtesy of Ossipee Historical Society

Lucy Howe Crawford as she appeared in the 1860s.

The falls of the Ammonoosuc River on the road to Franconia and Littleton. This lithograph by Isaac Sprague was made for William Oakes' Scenery of the White Mountains.

A lithograph of the White Mountains as seen from the Giant's Grave near the Mount Washington House in Crawford Notch. It was produced in 1848 by Isaac Sprague for William Oakes' Scenery of the White Mountains.

The Willey House in Crawford Notch. Courtesy of New Hampshire Historical Society

Coach, team, and passengers were all from the Strawberry Hill House in Bethlehem, New Hampshire. Courtesy of New Hampshire Historical Society

The Littleton & Profile II coach and six transporting tourists to their favorite vacation resort in the late 1800s. Courtesy of New Hampshire Historical Society

A post card of sightseers strolling past Sawyer's Rock on the Mountain Road between Bartlett and Bemis. From the author's collection

The White Mountains, All Aboard, *an engraving from* Harper's Weekly *dated August 13, 1859. Courtesy of New Hampshire Historical Society*

The disaster of 1826 left the Crawfords with fields, barns, and mills destroyed and half of their livestock gone. The road through the notch was almost completely washed out, and only two of thirty bridges remained in place. The Crawfords and their neighbors, with funds supplied from Portland, worked day and night to open the road. The businessmen of Portland made a two thousand dollar contribution of cash toward the reconstruction of the Tenth New Hampshire Turnpike because it was responsible for much economic development in Portland. The Maine legislature appropriated three thousand dollars for the project. One of many turnpikes chartered in the 1800s, the Tenth New Hampshire followed a route "from the upper line in Bartlett through the Notch in the white hills, containing twenty miles." This furnished a route to the seaports and became one of the best-paying turnpikes in northern New Hampshire. In winter, lines of teams from Coos, over a half a mile in length, were often seen on the road. Tough Canadian horses, harnessed to pungs or sleighs, were loaded with potash (or pearlash), butter, cheese, pork, lard, and peltry. They returned with assorted loads of merchandise for North Country residents. The teamsters were determined men engaged in the bonebreaking task of teaming freight over the hundred miles of dusty roads. Few

women or children made the trip. To those who did pass, luxuries were unknown, and the journey was made in the jolting discomfort of the wagons.

The Crawfords earned much of their money working on the roads and managing White Mountain property owned by nonresident proprietors. As the fame of the mountain scenery began to grow, coaches, arrived with visitors who required more conveniences than were provided for the hardy teamsters. Abel Crawford was known as "the patriarch of the mountains." His establishment was at the south end of the notch, near what is now called Bemis. His son, Thomas J. Crawford, ran the Notch House. Another son, Ethan Allen Crawford, was known as "the giant of the mountains." He operated an inn near Fabyan. Some tourists were as interested in the Crawfords as they were the mountains. Wealthy adventurers, writers, artists, scientists, and politicians all made the trip to see these New Hampshire folk heroes. Abel Crawford lived to be eighty-five years old, and he remained vigorous until the end. In the last decade of his life he greeted hundreds of visitors on his front porch and told stories about his beloved mountains. The old man with shaggy white hair and beard, a tame black bear by his side, was a true picture of a pioneer who had spent his life accumulating memories to share on these occasions.

THE MAKING OF POTASH

Most of the early settlers made potash, one of the few products that they could sell in Portsmouth or Portland to obtain money for supplies that they couldn't produce themselves. Potash, pearlash, or "salts" was made when land was cleared and the trees were reduced to ashes. The ashes were put in a tub and water allowed to trickle through into a hollow trough placed below. This liquid was boiled in a big iron kettle until it made a thick black fluid called salts. Sometimes it was boiled until it became a solid salt, dissolved in clean water, and boiled again. The second boiling produced a clean white powder, which served as baking powder for cooking.

An engraving of the Notch House in Crawford Notch by Fenner, Sears & Company, after a painting by Thomas Cole. Courtesy of New Hampshire Historical Society

TAMING A SABLE

William Crawford once found a live sable in one of his traps. The sable was in good condition and William decided to take it home to see if it would attack rats that infested the house. He put the sable head-down into a mitten and tucked it into his pocket. The little fellow was warm and comfortable and he completed the trip without incident.

A two- or three-foot cord was tied around his neck and he ate anything that was offered. He was put in the cellar where he soon cleared out the rats. The experiment ended when he gnawed off the string leaving a length of cord around his neck. He climbed to a window that was cracked a little, made a hole through it, and escaped. They found him dead in a trap next to the one in which he was first caught. The cord was still around his neck.

That fall the Crawfords caught about seventy-five of these sable for which they received nearly a dollar apiece. In the words of Ethan Allen Crawford, "We felt quite satisfied with our work."

Taming a Sable. *Illustration by Ron White*

A VISIT FROM DANIEL WEBSTER

In the summer of 1831, the Crawfords had a great many visitors, including Daniel Webster, who was then a member of Congress. He asked Ethan to guide him up the mountain and showed great interest in the things that they saw along the way. At the summit he addressed the mountain as follows:

> Mount Washington, I have come a long distance, have toiled hard to arrive at your summit, and now you seem to give me a cold reception, for which I am extremely sorry, as I shall not have time enough to view this grand prospect which now lies before me, and nothing prevents but the uncomfortable atmosphere in which you reside!

They decended through a cold snowstorm with the snow freezing to their bodies. The trip provided a number of stories for Webster to relate to his friends who had remained at the house. Crawford noted that after Webster paid his bill, "He made me a handsome present of twenty dollars."

Portrait of Daniel Webster. Courtesy of University of New Hampshire Collection

Ethan Allen Crawford described his association with a botanist in Lucy Crawford's *History of the White Mountains:*

> About this time (1825) a botanist came, who was making a collection of the plants of the White Mountains, as he could obtain here some rare ones, such as are not to be found elsewhere in America. I accompanied him on some of his tours around the mountains, and learned the different plants and names, and the different places where they grew. He went three times up and around the hills and staid some weeks with us.

During the summer of 1830 Crawford commented:

> I went up the mountain by an express desire from a botanist, to collect plants and save them alive, for I had been there so many times with a botanist to collect plants, that I had acquired considerable knowledge of plants, and the different places where they grew. I went over the hills and came down into the gulf, and then selected different species, such as now grow nowwhere else except in the cold climate of Greenland. I carefully took them up with a small quantity of earth and brought them home, placed them in a small vase with moist moss to preserve them, and then labeled the vase and sent it immediately to Boston. It was safely conveyed, and the plants were placed in a botanical garden; how many of them survived I cannot tell, as I never heard from them afterward.

The Crawford House and Mount Crawford from Oakes' Scenery of the White Mountains.

47

Loggers posed for this picture on the river bank. Many White Mountain streams were too narrow and rocky for river drives, and some areas remained uncut until logging railways were built to haul the logs to the mills. Courtesy of New Hampshire Historical Society

3
THE LOGGING INDUSTRY

All land grants made by representatives of the British Crown reserved the rights to all white and other pine trees suitable for masting. Ships were needed for trade with Europe and the West Indies. The Crown sought to preserve the best of the big white pines to be used as masts. They were blazed with the mark of a broad arrow, and heavy fines were levied if the trees were cut without permission. As the settlers moved deep into the mountain regions, a bitter struggle developed over the right of the royal governors to control the cutting of these big pines. The surveyor general seized timber at the mills, fined violators, and attempted to protect the crown's interests. However, there was great risk involved, and the surveyor's men were often beaten by mobs. After the Revolution, the law was abolished and mast cutting became a major industry.

Tremendous pines, two hundred feet high and six feet at the butt, were felled on a blanket of small trees and branches to deaden the fall. Long teams of oxen dragged the logs on sledges or pulled them suspended on an axle between two enormous wheels. Teams of oxen were also yoked at the rear to prevent the log from sliding too fast on the downgrade. "Mast roads" led to river banks, where the huge logs were floated to sea.

Before the Revolution, the king of England claimed all white pine trees large enough to use for masts in the Royal Navy. The king's representatives inspected mill yards and wood lots for trees and logs that were considered the property of the king. These were marked with the "King's Broad Arrow," a mark made with three blows of a hatchet. Some of these pines grew to enormous size, and moving them with ox teams was a difficult and dangerous task. One pine in Dunstable was recorded as having a butt that was 7 feet, 8 inches in diameter. Another pine in Lancaster was 264 feet in height. Mast roads were constructed so that these huge logs could be moved with sleds or giant wheels to the waterfront. They were then shipped to England and the West Indies in ships that were specially designed for the purpose.

The choppers arrived after "swampers" had cleared the area of brush, and a "bed" of branches was arranged to cushion the fall of the mast tree. Photo by Ron Bergeron

Many mast trees were damaged when they crashed to the ground. Once the tree was down, limbs were removed so that it could be hauled out by ox teams. Photo by Ron Bergeron

A chopping platform was built to position the choppers for the proper cut. Photo by Ron Bergeron

The masts were suspended from pairs of large wheels or rolled onto sleds. Photo by Ron Bergeron

Ox teams were moved into position and attached to the sleds or wheels. Photo by Ron Bergeron

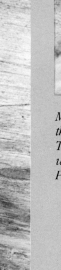

Masts were dragged through the forest to the nearest river and floated to the coast. They were sent to English shipyards for use on naval and merchant vessels. Photo by Ron Bergeron

"Cant dogs" were used to roll the heavy masts into position. Photo by Ron Bergeron

From a Kilburn Brothers stereoview documenting the success of two deer hunters in the late 1800s. The image was labeled Our Christmas Hunt. *Courtesy of New Hampshire Historical Society*

A White Mountains sawmill in full operation. From a stereograph by the Kilburn Brothers of Littleton, New Hampshire. Courtesy of New Hampshire Historical Society

A small sawmill of the type that was moved to the wood lot being cut, circa 1890. Courtesy of Ossipee Historical Society

The logs were sawed into boards that were transported from the sawmill by horses and oxen. This well-groomed team of horses has brought the boards to an open area where they will be stacked for future use. Courtsy of Ossipee Historical Society

The dense forest provided timber, fuel, and wild game. As the settlements began to grow, sawmills were built on many rivers and streams. Successful sawyers expanded their operations by purchasing timberland or stumpage. Mill companies were formed, and by 1852 Berlin had a dozen small mills. Dams were built along the rivers to provide the power for these mills.

The state contributed to the reduction of the forests by granting timberlands to schools, colleges, churches, and railroads. The state also sold timberland to obtain funds for roads and public buildings. In 1831 the land commissioner sold one tract of 33,941 acres for $1,023 and another tract of 10,000 acres for $300. In 1867 the state began selling its White Mountain forests to lumber companies at these ridiculously low prices. Approximately 17,200 acres were sold to local landowners and speculators for $25,000.

The railroad came of age during the Civil War, and by the mid-1870s rail lines were coming into the mountains from three different directions. The Concord & Montreal Railroad, later the Boston & Maine, came from the south through Concord and Woodsville. The Portland & Ogdensburg Railroad, later the Maine Central came from Portland, Maine, in the southeast. The Atlantic & St. Lawrence Railroad, later the Grand Trunk, came from Montreal and Portland in the north and east. Many of New Hampshire's rivers and streams were too rocky or shallow for log drives, and it was difficult to conduct large-scale operations in some of the mountain areas. Once the main rail lines were established, smaller logging railroads began to radiate into the river valleys. Horse teams twitched the logs to railroad sidings where they were loaded on cars and transported to the mills. Lumber was picked up by a major carrier or transported on the logging

NOTICE TO
Rail Road
CONTRACTORS!

Sealed proposals for building the sub-structure of the first 20 miles of the White Mountains Rail Road, from Woodsville to Littleton Village, will be received by the Directors of said Road, until *Tuesday, the 4th day of March next,*—Also for furnishing the Sleepers—furnishing the material and building the fences, and building the Depots—at which time the Directors will meet at *Lisbon Village,* and confer with parties wishing to contract.

Said contracts will be made payable one-half, at least, in the Stock of the Corporation, and the balance in Cash.

                                   W. H. CUMMINGS, *Clerk.*

Lisbon, February 18, 1851.

Notice to railroad contractors! Courtesy of New Hampshire Historical Society

Building railroads in the White Mountains frequently involved blasting through narrow openings between rock ledges. From a Kilburn Brothers stereograph. Courtesy of New Hampshire Historical Society

ENGLISH JACK—THE CRAWFORD NOTCH HERMIT

John Alfred Vials (or Viles) spent his summers in a shanty situated near the highway above the Gate of the Notch. He was known as "English Jack, the Hermit of the White Mountains" or the "Crawford Notch Hermit," and his old shanty became known as "the House that Jack Built." He derived considerable revenue from the sale of picture post-cards and other souvenirs, including a booklet containing his biography. Jack was born in London, orphaned at twelve, went to sea as a cabin boy, and was the only survivor of a shipwreck in the Indian Ocean. He later joined the navy and saw a great deal of action. Tiring of navy life, Jack came to America and drifted up to Crawford Notch to work on the railroad. He liked the region and decided to stay. Winters were spent hunting and trapping and making souvenirs to sell to summer visitors. As he grew older, he spent his winters with a family at Twin Mountain.

His shanty, which he called a ship, soon became a tourist attraction and Vials erected signs directing them to its location. English Jack died in April 1912 at the age of ninety.

Old Jack of the Mountain, White Mountains, N.H.

A post card showing "English Jack," the Crawford Notch hermit, and "the house that Jack built." From the author's collection

Railroad tracks through Crawford Notch, circa 1890. Courtesy of Ossipee Historical Society

A train passing through the gates of Crawford Notch with the hotel in the background. From a stereograph by B. W. Kilburn. From the author's collection

Loggers relax in front of their mountain cabin while the cook and housekeeper watches from the doorway. Courtesy of New Hampshire Historical Society

railroad to a connection with a major carrier that profited by taking the goods to market. At least seventeen logging railroads were built to take logs to company-owned sawmills.

In the 1880s, the sulfite processing of reducing softwoods to pulp was introduced. Coupled with the completion of the major rail lines into the White Mountains, sulfite processing meant that immense profits could be made by harvesting the conifers. Logging company owners such as J. E. Henry, the Saunders family, and George Van Dyke moved quickly to acquire small plots of privately owned land. Land companies were formed to acquire large tracts of forest and farmlands. The New Hampshire Land Company was responsible for depopulating the entire farming village of Thornton

Gore. It also acquired large tracts in Benton, Easton, Ellsworth, Woodstock, Warren, Lincoln, and Thornton. Once the land was acquired, it was sold or leased only to logging or paper companies in lots of ten thousand acres or more.

Early logging camps were usually rustic affairs constructed of logs for temporary shelter. Each camp had a cookshack and dining area, a poorly ventilated and crowded bunkhouse, a stable and blacksmith shop, an outhouse, and an office. A few of the camps had frame buildings that could be moved to a new location when the adjacent lot had been completely cut over.

W. R. Brown, from Portland, bought a Berlin lumber operation in 1869. At first he devoted his energy to selling lumber shipped to Portland. Then he moved to Berlin,

THE NEW HAMPSHIRE LAND COMPANY

Summer visitors to this section of the White Mountains have noticed the many deserted farms and dilapidated buildings and have wondered at such scenes, not dreaming that the cause was to be found in the operations of a company *chartered to do it*; that this desolation was due to the gradual tightening of coils of a boa constrictor *legalized* to crush the human life out of these regions, preparatory to stripping them of their forests; for depopulation here is not due to causes which have led to the abandonment of farms elsewhere in the state. The inhabitants of this section have never depended upon the scant return of rough farms for a living but rather upon their winter's work in the woods, a dependence that never would have been exhausted had they been left in possession, since their methods were those which are now advocated by scientific forestry. The farmer felled some of the largest trees in the woods every winter and hauling them out endwise injured nothing but left the rest better for it.

"His successor, the professional lumberman, cuts everything, rolls it down the mountain, crushing the saplings, and not content with that, often burns the refuse for charcoal. The Land Company has boasted that extensive lumber operations could never have been undertaken in this section without its assistance in paving the way—an assistance which in one instance they say involved the preliminary acquisition of sixty different titles.

"The White Mountain wilderness is the last considerable one in New Hampshire, the tide of agricultural improvement having long ago surged around it and swept northward leaving untouched, until the Land Company could get its preliminary work upon it, this grand natural park out of whose heart gushes the Merrimack, which flows the whole length of the state and is the main artery of its economic life. This region is unrivaled for natural beauty this side of the Rockies, and may well be called the Switzerland of America.

"The tide of travel to it for health and recreation is an ever-increasing one. The governor of New Hampshire in a recent message estimated the natural expenditure of tourists at over five million dollars. In view of this fact and the further one that the Merrimack is gradually dwindling, to the great detriment of the manufactories that line its banks, it is amazing that the process of denuding this upper region of its forests in the most wasteful manner has not been arrested, or at least hindered, long ago, and it probably would have been but for the fact that the whole business is largely in the hands of an unscrupulous and merciless corporation—a Trust of the most concentrated, ruthless and soulless character, which is bent on reducing the entire section to a blackened, hideous, howling wilderness."

From a presentation called The Boa Constrictor of the White Mountains or the Worst "Trust" in the World, *presented by Rev. John E. Johnson, North Woodstock, New Hampshire, July 4, 1900.*

Clear-cutting left this woman and her three children living in a barren and desolate area. From a Kilburn Brothers stereograph. Courtesy of New Hampshire Historical Society

---

THE

BOA CONSTRICTOR OF THE WHITE MOUNTAINS

OR

THE WORST "TRUST" IN THE WORLD.

What is it? The New Hampshire Land Company.
Where is it? Up among the granite hills of that state.
What is its object? To deforest and depopulate the region lying around the head waters of the Merrimack river in the heart of the White Mountains.
It's history and *modus operandi*? In the early days of the company it was allowed to acquire for a song all the public lands thereabouts, and later to "take over" all tax-titles, until finally there were no considerable tracts in that vicinity which it did not own.

Title page from the pamphlet by the Reverend John E. Johnson protesting the actions of the New Hampshire Land Company. The pamphlet was dated July 4, 1900. Courtesy of University of New Hampshire Special Collections

where he acquired or built pulp and lumber mills. His logging crew operated in vast areas, including sections of Maine.

In Whitefield, two other men named Brown bought twenty-six thousand acres of pine, at fifty cents per acre, and logged the majestic forests in Jefferson and Randolph. They operated a dozen sawmills in the Whitefield area and eventually increased their production to twenty-three million feet per year. In 1903 they sold their holdings to Cassius Twitchell, a political boss who controlled vast areas of forestland.

George Van Dyke made his first big move when he beat Brown of Berlin to cutting rights in the Dartmouth grants. The 260-pound timber baron cut millions of feet

of virgin spruce and shipped it out by river and rail. He drove a team of fast horses in order to keep track of his workmen. He drove so fast, in fact, that he killed team after team. Eventually local land owners had to attach his equipment in order to collect damages caused by his log drives.

J. E. Henry was the timber king of the Pemigewasset Valley. J. E. Had been a horse trader, a Canadian oilman, and teamster before he moved to Newbury, Vermont, where he bought a wood lot. He bought several lots near Woodsville from which he removed wood and timber. Failed ventures in a wheat farm in Minnesota, a California ranch, and some gold mines left him in poor financial condition. In 1890 he joined George Van Dyke and

Brown's Lumber Company mills in Whitefield from an engraving by Van Slyck & Company of Boston. Courtesy of New Hampshire Historical Society

bought seventy thousand acres of spruce and pine in the Pemigewasset Wilderness. When the survey showed a billion feet of lumber, Henry bought out Van Dyke for $100,000. He moved his wife into Lincoln and built a village of green lumber on the stumps of trees just felled.

The hard-driving lumber baron eventually established a dozen or more logging camps. He tried to drive logs down the East Branch of the Pemigewasset by building dams on the river. When this failed, he built a railroad to haul the logs and lumber. His three sons built a pulp mill in 1898 and a paper mill in 1902 to use the smaller trees that remained after the big spruce and pine had been stripped from the wood lots. Norwegians, Russians, and Poles were met on the docks in Boston and

recruited to work in the mills. After Henry's death in 1912, his sons lived lavishly. By 1917 they were in financial difficulties and were forced to sell to Parker and Young of Lisbon.

Lincoln is an example of a mill village that survived. Zealand—with a sawmill, railroad station, school, store, post office, houses, car shops, and charcoal kilns—existed from 1881 to 1904. Other villages like Livermore, Johnson, and Carrigain lasted only as long as the logging operation was active. Once the forest was cleared or burned, or the mill destroyed or abandoned, these villages simply disappeared.

Piles of pulpwood accumulated near a New Hampshire mill in 1925. Photograph by Francis Wagner. Courtesy of University of New Hampshire Media Services

Drivers with their teams stop by a river clogged with logs. Courtesy of New Hampshire Historical Society

This View on the Pemigewasset *illus-trated an article written about "The Summer Tourist" published in* Harper's Magazine *in 1852.*

A group of loggers pose on the river bank during a log drive, possibly on the Connecticut River. Courtesy of New Hampshire Historical Society

TOURISM

Meanwhile, the second generation of innkeepers was beginning to respond to a need for more genteel accommodations for the increasing flow of visitors. Horace Fabyan took over Ethan Allen Crawford's property in 1837 and purchased the Willey House in 1844. He constructed a two-and-a-half story addition to the Willey House, sold it, and built a three-story addition to Crawford's old inn, which he renamed the Mount Washington House. It was probably the largest hotel in the White Mountains when it was completed in 1848. The Flume House and the Lafayette House in Franconia Notch were under construction at this time.

The new railroads had a tremendous impact on the flow of visitors into the White Mountain region. Where hundreds had come before, now thousands came. By 1851 the Atlantic and St. Lawrence Railroad connected Gorham with Portland, Maine. Tourists could now travel to within eight miles of Mount Washington by train. At that time, there were only five public houses from which the summit of the mountain could be reached in a day. The Boston, Concord & Montreal Railroad went from Concord or Bow to Sanbornton in 1848, to Plymouth in 1850 and Wells River in 1853, to Lancaster in 1870, to Groveton in 1872, and to Fabyan in 1874. Two years later the railroad was extended from Fabyan to the base station of the cog railway. In 1879 a narrow-gauge line was opened to the Profile House and another reached Bethlehem in 1881. The Profile and Franconia Notch Railroad was changed to standard gauge in 1897. Branch lines connected North Woodstock to Plymouth in 1883, and Berlin was connected to the Whitefield & Jefferson Railroad ten years later. A spur, opened in 1892, reached the Waumbek Hotel.

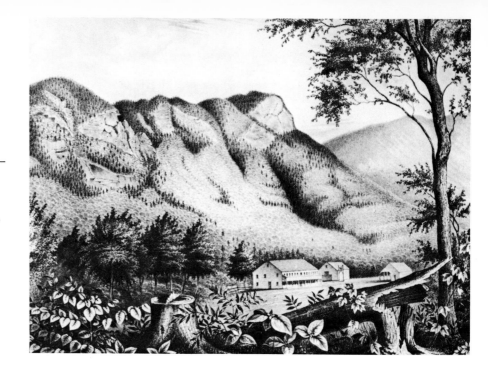

Isaac Sprague's 1848 lithograph of Franconia Notch and the Lafayette House was produced for William Oakes' Scenery of the White Mountains.

A train on the tracks at the Mount Crawford House, circa 1887. The photogravure is from Thomas Starr King's The White Hills: Their Legends, Landscape, and Poetry.

Cover of a Concord and Montreal Railroad guidebook to New Hampshire resorts. The expanding railroad systems played a major role in the expansion of the tourist industry in the White Mountains. Courtesy of New Hampshire Historical Society

THE MERRIMACK VALLEY ROUTE

Concord and Montreal Railroad.

Summer Excursions TO THE Lake and Mountain Resorts of New Hampshire AND CANADA, with HOTEL AND BOARDING HOUSE LISTS.

BOSTON PASSENGER AGENCY
207 WASHINGTON ST.

Ranlet's Hotel in Bethlehem from an original stereograph by G. H. Aldrich of Littleton. Courtesy of New Hampshire Historical Society

BOSTON AND MAINE RAILROAD
SUMMER EXCURSIONS TO THE
WHITE MOUNTAINS · MT · DESERT ·
WINNIPESAUKEE RANGELEY AND MOOSEHEAD LAKES AND THE New England Beaches
Routes · Rates · Maps ·
Hotel & Boarding House List
Etc · Etc ·

An 1888 Boston & Maine Railroad guidebook to the White Mountains of New Hampshire and Mount Desert Island on the Maine coast. Courtesy of New Hampshire Historical Society

The Lincoln House in Bethlehem. Notice the large garden in the foreground. Courtesy of New Hampshire Historical Society

The Glen House near the entrance to the Mount Washington Auto Road. Courtesy of New Hampshire Historical Society

Guests at the Crawford House "mounting up" to climb Mount Washington, circa 1890. Courtesy of New Hampshire Historical Society

Gorham's population increased significantly between 1850 and 1860. The Alpine House had been built by the Atlantic & St. Lawrence Railroad to accommodate the first loads of passengers in 1851, and Joseph M. Thompson was operating the Glen House, which had rooms for two hundred guests. This grand resort hotel was destroyed by fire in 1884 and replaced by a more modern version. As the railroads expanded, so did the large hotels. In fact, there were railroad stations at the Crawford House, the Fabyan House, and the Mount Pleasant House. The Profile House had its own narrow gauge railway, and the Pemigewasset House was built by the

Boston, Concord & Montreal Railroad. Bethlehem advertised that its climate would prove beneficial to hay fever sufferers and it became a major vacation center. In 1879 the town boasted twenty-four hotels that could accommodate 1,450 guests. The last of the grand hotels was the Mount Washington Hotel, opened in Bretton Woods in 1902. Constructed at a cost of 1.5 million dollars, the giant structure combined modern conveniences with architectural excellence. Of the many hotels built in Crawford Notch, the Mount Washington is the only one still standing.

THE FABYAN HOUSE

Capt. Eleazar Rosebrook, a veteran of the Revolutionary War, built a farmhouse and mill near a mound called the Giant's Grave, in 1792. Twenty-five years later, he bequeathed the property to his grandson, Ethan Allen Crawford, "the giant of the hills." Ethan, a famous guide and hunter, often entertained travelers in his house, and led them to the summit of Mount Washington. He kept an inn from 1803 to 1819, but the Rosebrook house was burned and two others met the same fate.

Horace Fabyan eventually acquired the property and erected the largest hotel in the White Mountains, with over one hundred rooms. Fabyan's hotel, the White Mountain House, was destroyed by fire in 1853. The new hotel, constructed in the 1880s, accommodated five hundred guests, had convenient connections to both the Portland and Ogdensburgh and the Boston, Concord and Montreal railroads, had a beautiful view of the Presidential Range and was about ten miles from the summit of Mount Washington.

Cover for the Fayban House menu during the summer of 1883. Courtesy of New Hampshire Historical Society

Menu from Fabyan's Hotel in 1883. Courtesy of New Hampshire Historical Society

Dining room at the Fabyan House. "We await your pleasure." Courtesy of New Hampshire Historical Society

Mount Washington from the Fabyan House in the late 1800s. From an original Kilburn Brothers stereograph. Courtesy of New Hampshire Historical Society

The Fabyan Hotel staff in the dining room, circa 1892. Courtesy of New Hampshire Historical Society

Profile House from Bald Mountain with artist sketching the dramatic scenery. Courtesy of New Hampshire Historical Society

This advertisement from an unknown issue of Among the Clouds *emphasizes that Bethlehem was free from hay fever and that Sinclair Hotel guests had access to a new 18-hole golf links and clubhouse. Courtesy of New Hampshire Historical Society*

Mount Pleasant House at Fabyan's in the White Mountains. Courtesy of New Hampshire Historical Society

BETHLEHEM AND THE MAPLEWOOD HOTEL

One of the most popular summer resorts in the White Mountains is the village of Bethlehem, which is located on a high plateau on the west side of the Presidential Range, and beyond the Ammonoosuc Valley. The village, 1,450 feet above sea level, gets cool breezes from one direction and a magnificent view of the White Mountains from the other. The cool, sweet air of Bethlehem attracted hundreds of visitors. The Sinclair House accommodated more than three hundred guests, and the Maplewood Hotel was expanded from a boardinghouse to an immense hotel located about midway between the village of Bethlehem and the railroad station. The view of the Presidential Range is especially beautiful at sunset. A short walk to Crufts' Ledge provided a panoramic view of the Franconia Mountains across the forest-covered valley of the Gale River.

White Mts. N.H. Bethlehem, Park Street toward Golf Links.

Park Street in Bethlehem, New Hampshire. This was the route to the new golf links and clubhouse. From the author's collection

White Mts., N.H. The Maplewood, Bethlehem.

The Maplewood Hotel was one of the many large hotels that made Bethlehem a very popular White Mountain summer resort. From the author's collection

The Sinclair Hotel was a haven for hay fever sufferers in the White Mountains. From the author's collection

A sketch of the Summit House on Mount Washington from Incidents in White Mountain History, *by Benjamin G. Willey, published in 1856.*

A more recent post card view of the Glen House. From the author's collection

The Mount Washington Hotel on a 2,600-acre private preserve in Bretton Woods. A grand resort hotel with 235 rooms and scenic golf course.

The Summit House, constructed as a direct result of existing or anticipated railroad advances toward the White Mountains, was the first hostelry built on Mount Washington. During the summer of 1852, Nathan R. Perkins of Jefferson and Lucius M. Rosebrook and Joseph R. Hall of Lancaster, constructed the crude building from local stone and lumber carried up the mountain on the backs of horses. Two boards were carried on each side of the horse while the drivers walked behind and carried the ends of the boards. Mr. Rosebrook is reputed to have carried the front door on his back from the Glen House. The stones were secured to the ledge with cement and iron rods. The wooden roof was secured with four stout cables. Inside the building was a stove, a table that would accommodate thirty or forty people, and a row of beds separated by curtains. After 1854 the Summit House was used only as sleeping quarters.

The Tip-Top House was built by Samuel Fitch Spaulding in 1853. It was also built of stones and had a deck roof where visitors could view the scenery in pleasant weather. Because supplies had to be brought up on horseback, fresh foods were not on the menu. Food preparation was complicated because the staff had no way of knowing how many people would come up the mountain each day. One manager of the Tip-Top House reported that he estimated the number of dinner guests by counting the ponies on the bridle path from Crawford's.

"We are where the breezes blow today," was the message from this visitor to the summit of Mount Washington in 1906. From the author's collection

An early post card view of the Tip-Top House on Mount Washington. From the author's collection

The Tip-Top House in winter. From the author's collection

THE SNOW ARCH

The water that runs from Tuckerman's Ravine passes under the great snow bank and cuts a deep channel, which forms a snow arch. On July 16, 1854, D. O. Macomber, president of the Mount Washington Carriage Road, C. H. V. Cavis, road engineer, and writer John H. Spaulding dined in that snow arch. At that time it was 266 feet long, 84 feet wide, and 40 feet high. Icy water constantly dripped from the roof, but the snow sheltered them from a heavy thundershower which passed over the area.

Under the great snow arch in Tuckerman's ravine. From a stereograph by B. W. Kilburn taken on August 15, 1879. From the author's collection

Top House On Mt. Washington In Winter.

Looking down the Mount Washington Carriage Road. From a stereograph by John P. Soule taken at the Ledge. From the author's collection

The first horse and buggy was driven to the summit of Mount Washington by J. M. Thompson on July 13, 1861. From a stereograph by John P. Soule. From the author's collection

Gen. David O. Macomber was granted a charter for the White Mountain Road Company in 1853. He proposed to build a sixteen-foot-wide macadam road with three-foot-high protective walls in the dangerous places. It would lead to a grand hotel on the summit of the mountain. Surveyors were instructed to lay out the most picturesque route. They placed the road almost exactly where it is located today. The route was eight miles long with an average grade of 12 percent and a maximum grade of 26 percent. A contract was awarded for construction at $8,000 per mile and work began in 1854.

The site was eight miles from the nearest railroad, so

This view of the base station of the cog railway shows several of the buildings and a Concord coach. A Kilburn Brothers photograph. Courtesy of New Hampshire Historical Society

all supplies had to be hauled by horses and oxen. Holes for blasting were hand-drilled and blasting was done with black powder. The project ran out of funds when the road reached the ledge just above the Halfway House in 1857. No new financial backers could be found and for three years the carriage road lay half completed. Twelve partially finished omnibuses of special design were also victims of the financial collapse.

In 1859 a new corporation was formed. It had the financial backing of David Pingree, who controlled large areas of forest land on the southerly side of Mount Washington and woodland believed to include the summit.

The directors of the old company released their interest in the roadbed and right of way. On July 6, 1860, the toll road was opened from the Glen House to the ledge above the Halfway House, and Joseph S. Hall, the contractor, completed the road during the following summer. Col. Joseph Thompson, owner of the Glen House, drove a one-horse buckboard to the top in June before the road was finished. He thus drove the first vehicle to the summit ahead of his rival, Col. John Hitchcock, owner of the Alpine House in Gorham.

A post card showing Old Peppersass *making its last trip up the Mount Washington cog railway. From the author's collection*

Old Peppersass *and crew on the cog railway trestle. A Kilburn Brothers photograph. Courtesy of New Hampshire Historical Society*

Cog railway passengers crossed a trestle bridge on a trip to the summit of Mount Washington. From the author's collection

From that time, nearly every White Mountain hotel operated a mountain wagon, and a tour to the summit was a feature of every White Mountain vacation. The drive usually took a full day and included a look at the view through a telescope from the flat roof of the Tip Top House. The first recorded fatal accident on the Mount Washington Summit Road occurred on July 12, 1880, when a four-horse mountain wagon was overturned by an intoxicated driver. One passenger was killed and the driver, it is said, eventually died from his injuries. During that first summer, one hundred horse-drawn vehicles used the carriage road. The road was later widened and improved and, in 1930, four thousand automobiles drove to the summit. The old carriage road became known as the automobile road and bumper stickers announced, "This car climbed Mount Washington."

In 1858 Sylvester Marsh petitioned the New Hampshire legislature for a charter to build a railroad up to the summit of Mount Washington. The legislators did not take him seriously because it seemed such an impossible enterprise, but they did grant charters for railways up Mount Washington and Mount Lafayette. It has been said that an amendment was proposed to permit him to build a railway to the moon.

Marsh was a tinkerer whose invention of meat-packing machinery brought him a fortune that was lost in the panic of the 1830s. He regained his fortune in the grain business and retired at age fifty-two. According to one account, he got his idea for a cog railway from Herrick Aiken, a Franklin resident. Aiken is said to have showed Marsh a model of the roadbed and track with cog rail that he had built as early as 1850. Marsh's challenge was to design a steam engine that would climb a steep grade and descend safely. He invested five hundred dollars of his own funds in a model engine, a car, and twenty feet of track. His demonstrations impressed investors and he raised enough money to organize the Mount Washington Steam Railway Company in 1865.

Marsh selected a route established by the early trail-makers, Ethan Allen Crawford and Horace Fabyan. He had an area cleared for the train station, boarding house, and other buildings that would be required to support the project. The nearest railroad station was twenty-five miles away in Littleton and all materials and supplies had to be hauled by ox teams to the construction site. The workmen cut logs on the site and built a log cabin to house them while they were in the wilderness. They widened Fabyan's road to the base of the mountain and sawed logs into timbers to support the rails.

The first locomotive reached Littleton in sections and had to be hauled by ox teams to the base station. A blacksmith shop was created and the locomotive was assembled. It was christened *Hero* but the upright boiler caused people to call it *Old Peppersass* because it looked like a peppersauce bottle, and the name stuck. A quarter-mile of track was built in the summer of 1866. This included a trestle bridge across the Ammonoosuc River at a grade of seventeen hundred feet to a mile. On August 28, *Old*

Peppersass moved a platform car and forty passengers up and down the new track. The demonstration received great publicity and Marsh received much-needed pledges of financial support.

A half-mile of track was laid in 1867 and the great trestle called Jacob's Ladder was built in 1868. The track was now three-quarters of a mile from the summit, and fifty guests made the trip propelled by a new locomotive called the *George Stephenson*. The passengers completed their journey on foot and dined at the Tip Top House. Attempts to complete the railway before winter were unsuccessful, but on July 3, 1869, the first train reached the summit.

Walter Aiken, the son of investor Herrick Aiken, eventually took control of the railway. Marsh continued as president for many years, but his authority over company operations was rather quickly usurped. Although a clever investor and businessman, Marsh was unsuccessful in his attempts to regain control. Aiken knew everything about the railway and its equipment. He was an extremely competent manager who could and did make repairs when the occasion demanded.

The Marshfield House was constructed at the base in 1871. It was operated by E. K. Cox and used by stage drivers before the railroad was extended from Fabyan to the base in 1876. A new terminal was constructed at the base, and the cog railway added a half-mile of track to connect with the new line. Fabyan became the busiest spot in the mountains at train time. Many tourists took the cog railway up the mountain and came down the carriage road by stage to the Glen House. They would return to Fabyan on the train through the notch in the late afternoon.

A new Mount Washington Summit House was built on the mountain in 1873 and 1874. The large building could sleep 100 people and the dining room could seat 150. Built at a cost of seventy thousand dollars, the construction materials had to be hauled up the mountain by rail, one car at a time. The two stone houses were converted to lodging for employees of the hotel and the cog railway. In 1885 the old Summit House was torn down and replaced by a wooden dormitory.

Slideboards, used by many of the workmen, were the most colorful way to come down the mountain. Three feet long and a foot wide, the boards fitted over the cog rails and were controlled with two friction-brake handles which checked the speed of the slide. The average slide-boarder made three miles in ten minutes. The record for three miles was two minutes and forty-five seconds.

A daily summer newspaper, *Among the Clouds*, began publication in 1877. Its founder was Henry M. Burt, who established his newspaper office in the front room of the old Tip Top House and employed a full-time staff of four with three part-time compositors. The equipment arrived on an open platform car pushed by a cog railway locomotive. It took the staff several days to set up the press. The first issue was printed late in the afternoon on July 18. It was soon learned that guests wanted a paper announcing their own arrivals, so two editions were

Base station and depot of the Mount Washington cog railway. Courtesy of New Hampshire Historical Society

In 1895 a fire destroyed the engine house, machine shops, and the depot at the base station of the cog railway. Two of the locomotives, *Eagle* and *Tip Top*, were extensively damaged and had to be rebuilt. By coincidence, another cog railway on Mount Desert Island had two locomotives that had been built by the Manchester Locomotive Works of Manchester, New Hampshire. They were identical to those built for the Mount Washington Cog Railway. The two locomotives were in storage because the Green Mountain system on Mount Desert had been put out of business by an auto road. They were acquired by the Mount Washington Railway and quickly pressed into service as No. 4 and No. 5 later changed to No. 3).

Jacob's Ladder trestle on the cog railway. Courtesy of New Hampshire Historical Society

An early stereoview by Charles Bierstadt shows the train and passengers near the summit of Mount Washington. Courtesy of James Dolph

A new Mount Washington Summit House was built to sleep one hundred people. Its dining room could seat 150. The original Summit House was eventually torn down and replaced by a wooden dormitory. Courtesy of New Hampshire Historical Society

FATALITIES ON THE COG RAILWAY

In spite of its dangerous route and the unpredictable weather on Mount Washington, the cog railway had a remarkable safety record. In fact, the first fatality was in 1929, when *Old Peppersass*, which had been recently rebuilt, was sent up the track as part of a celebration. With a large crowd on hand, it chugged to within a half-mile of the summit. As it started down, it hopped out of the cog rail and began descending at a faster and faster speed. Reverend Guy Roberts, who had "recovered" *Peppersass* from the Baltimore & Ohio Railroad, was stationed alongside Jacob's Ladder for the thrill of seeing *Peppersass* on its final journey. Instead, he was the closest witness to its fatal plunge. All the passengers but one jumped from the train. Daniel Rossiter, a publicity agent for the Boston & Maine, was killed when *Peppersass* left the tracks at Jacob's Ladder. Winston Pote, a well-known White Mountains photographer was seriously injured when he leaped from the engine.

Pote was quoted as saying, "Many photographers went up Mount Washington that day looking for special pictures. All of us missed the big one. However, I had the fastest ride on the slowest locomotive ever built, and lived to remember the last climb of Old Peppersass."

Before the summer was over, the original locomotive was reassembled in the Concord repair shops and eventually placed on display at the base station.

The most serious accident in the railway's history took place on September 17, 1967. The last train left the summit just before dark. The engine and car were both thrown off the cog rail as they passed over one of the siding switches. They quickly slid out of control and fell off the tracks. Rescue efforts were hampered by darkness. Eight people were killed and many were injured. A lengthy review of the accident determined that the switch had been improperly set, perhaps even tampered with by hikers or unauthorized personnel. All switches are now checked before trains pass over them to insure that railway passengers will have a safe trip to and from the summit.

The Base Station was damaged in a 1967 accident. It was hauled back to the tracks on a specially built runway and went down the mountain under its own power. Courtesy of Mount Washington Observatory Collection

The ill-fated Chumley car after the 1967 accident. Courtesy of Mount Washington Observatory Collection

The third Summit House built on Mount Washington also served as the cog railway depot on the mountaintop. From the author's collection

Slideboards were three feet long and one foot wide. The boards fitted over the cog rail and were controlled with two friction-brake handles which regulated the speed of the slide. Courtesy of Mount Washington Observatory Collection

This was the July 13, 1887 edition of Among the Clouds, *the newspaper printed on the summit of Mount Washington. Courtesy of New Hampshire Historical Society*

Slideboarding Among the Clouds *to the base for distribution to hotels in the White Mountain region. Courtesy of Mount Washington Observatory Collection*

BASE STATION NAMED MARSHFIELD

Reverend Guy Roberts, pastor of the Whitefield Methodist Episcopal Church, was responsible for the cog railway's base station being named Marshfield in 1926. He first got the idea from an old stereoscopic image of the Marshfield House, a large hotel built in 1871 at the bottom of the old railway, a quarter of a mile below the base station. The Marshfield House went out of business after twenty years of operation. It was used by tramps until it burned in 1896. Pastor Roberts felt that the hotel had been named in honor of Sylvester Marsh who had founded the cog railway. His wife suggested that the last half of the name could be considered in honor of

Darby Field, the first white man known to have climbed Mount Washington, in 1642. When Roberts suggested naming the base station Marshfield, all parties readily agreed that it was an appropriate way to honor Sylvester Marsh and Darby Field, two white mountain pioneers.

Peppersass, the world's first mountain-climbing locomotive, played a major role in the construction of the cog railway. A second engine, the *George Stephenson*, was added in 1868, and the two engines made many trips up and down the mountain until they were replaced by engines with horizontal boilers in 1878. The retired *Peppersass* was displayed in the 1893 World's Colum-

bian Exposition in Chicago and was on exhibit in the Field Museum of Natural History for ten years. In 1904, the *Peppersass* was sent to St. Louis for the Louisiana Purchase Exposition. Somehow, it came into the custody of the Baltimore & Ohio Railroad, which sent it to the Fair of the Iron Horse in 1928.

Reverend Roberts discovered the location of the historic engine and negotiated with the B & O to transfer it to the Boston & Maine Railroad, the operator of the cog railway. *Peppersass* was reconditioned in the B & M repair shops in Concord and returned to the cog railway area as a permanent tourist attraction.

The Marshfield House with Mount Washington in the background is seen in this original stereoview by the Kilburn Brothers. Courtesy of New Hampshire Historical Society

Henry M. Burt, editor of Among the Clouds *and an accomplished White Mountain photographer. Courtesy of Mount Washington Observatory Collection*

This cold weather scene at the United States Observatory on Mount Washington is from a Kilburn Brothers stereograph. From the author's collection

printed to include the noon arrivals and the early evening arrivals. The printing office quickly became a tourist attraction where many visitors saw their first printing press.

Eventually three reporters were hired each summer to gather news from Bethlehem, Bretton Woods, Fabyan, and North Conway. Slideboards were used to get the early morning edition down the mountain and in the hands of readers before the breakfast hour. Late-breaking stories could be filed by reporters who caught the last train for the summit and wrote their stories on the trip up the mountain. The papers were printed, folded, and bundled. At three o'clock in the morning they were handed to railway men on slideboards. Ten minutes later they were at the base. A wagon with a team of fast horses delivered them to Bethlehem or Fabyan where they were put on the first train going through Crawford Notch to North Conway.

Henry Burt was a well-regarded mountain photographer who toted a heavy five-by-seven view camera and glass plates all over the mountain top. Strong winds forced him to weight the tripod with heavy rocks to avoid having his equipment blown into some ravine. Burt once fell about thirty feet while trying to take a photograph of the headwall of Tuckerman's Ravine. He received injuries to his back from which he never completely recovered.

In May 1871 the United States Government established a weather bureau on the summit of Mount Washington and assigned members of the Army Signal Service to operate the station. They were quartered in the old railway building until a signal station was built for their use in 1874.

Church services were held in nearly all the White Mountain hotels, and a Sunday school was established on

The Mount Washington Signal Station. From a Kilburn Brothers stereograph. From the author's collection

This 1852 advertisement for the White Mountain House is from Tripp & Osgood's The White Mountain Guide. *Courtesy of University of New Hampshire Special Collections*

the summit of Mount Washington in 1877. Henry Ward Beecher spent his summers at the Twin Mountain House between 1871 and 1880. He conducted services there, and it was not uncommon for him to attract five hundred people to his services. On one occasion, in 1874, he had two thousand people in his congregation.

Improved rail service attracted wealthy tourists from all over the country and it became necessary for the hotels to provide more than fresh air and spectacular scenery. Their fashionable customers expected good food, comfortable accommodations, and excellent service. They also wanted entertainment. Scores of guidebooks were published over the years to direct tourists to boating, swimming, hiking, tennis, golf, archery, dances, lectures, card parties, concerts, and plays. Hotels introduced gas lighting in the 1870s and electric lights at the turn of the century.

The Sunset Hill House, annex, and cottages in the White Mountains, New Hampshire. From the author's collection

GIVEN AWAY
BY "THE WHITE MOUNTAIN ECHO."

SUMMER -
- HAUNTS

— AND —

Winter Retreats.

May be had FREE at the various Ticket and Tourist Offices in Boston, New York, Montreal, and other Cities, and mailed on receipt of two-cent stamp from the office of "THE WHITE MOUNTAIN ECHO," Bethlehem, N. H.

Title page from Summer Haunts and Winter Retreats, *a "give away" published by the* White Mountain Echo *in the 1890s. Courtesy of New Hampshire Historical Society*

They proudly announced the availability of a telegraph office and later described the number of telephones available to their guests. Eventually, it became important to announce the number of "water closets" that were added each season.

Many hotels promoted bicycling, and colorfully outfitted wheelmen flashed through mountain villages on their silver-plated machines. Tandem bicycling was introduced to the mountains in 1887 and became very popular. A smooth bicycle path was constructed between Plymouth and the Profile House in 1881. The Forest Hills House of Franconia built a quarter-mile track in 1884, the Sunset Hill House of Sugar Hill built a half-mile track in 1897, and the Profile House constructed a track in 1899. North Conway and Jackson constructed bike roads, a path was opened between the Crawford House and the Mount Pleasant House, and signs marking crossroads were erected by the League of American Wheelmen.

A post card view of the Crawford House and Saco Lake from Elephant's Head. From the author's collection

The Mount Pleasant Hotel in Bretton Woods. From the author's collection

During the 1880s and 1890s, many hotels added rifle ranges, roller skating rinks and casinos. The Maplewood Casino, which opened in 1888, had facilities for dancing, lectures, billiards, and bowling. Most hotels had tennis courts and sponsored tennis tournaments. Many had baseball teams made up of employees recruited from area colleges. A lively competition between the various hotels entertained both the employees and the tourists.

In the late 1890s golf became the most popular sport in the mountains. Golf links opened at the Maplewood and the town of Jackson in 1896, at the Mount Pleasant House in 1897, and in the towns of North Woodstock and Bethlehem in 1898. The Bethlehem Park and Fair Association operated the golf course for all hotel guests and an English greenskeeper was hired to care for the course.

Band concerts and outdoor evening plays were also popular. In 1885 Markinfield Addey, editor of the *Echo*, pushed the town of Bethlehem into forming the Bethle-hem Amusement Association and hiring a director of amusements. Addey wanted a "gala day" and one was planned for August 1885. Activities included baseball, lawn tennis, a tug of war, foot races, fireworks, and a fancy dress ball. The following year a gala day was scheduled each week with a grand gala day at the end of the season. In 1887 gala day was replaced by the Grand Annual Parade of the White Mountain Coaches. Twenty-seven brightly decorated stagecoaches participated in the parade, which was a great success. Forty-two coaches attracted over five thousand spectators in 1888 and in 1889, ten thousand people were in Bethlehem for the parade. By 1891, 130 coaches were watched by thousands of spectators and a Coaching Parade Association was established in 1893. The parades continued until 1898, when the expense became too great and the hotels could no longer support the program. Coaching parades were also held in Lancaster, Littleton, and North Conway. The 1895 parade in North

THE NINTH ANNUAL
White Mountain Coaching Parade!

A BRILLIANT PAGEANT!—THOUSANDS OF DELIGHTED SPECTATORS!

A FULL AND GRAPHIC DESCRIPTION OF THE GRAND EVENT.

"Whereso'er I Turn my Ravished Eyes,
Gay Gilded Scenes and Shining Prospects Rise."

The country club and golf links in Bethlehem was one of the many golf facilities built at the White Mountain resorts. From the author's collection

An elaborately decorated Concord coach with passengers dressed for the coaching parade. Courtesy of New Hampshire Historical Society

The Jackson Falls House coach and six with passengers dressed for the coaching parade. Courtesy of New Hampshire Historical Society

Mr. and Mrs. Freelan O. Stanley making the first ascent of Mount Washington by auto on August 30, 1899.

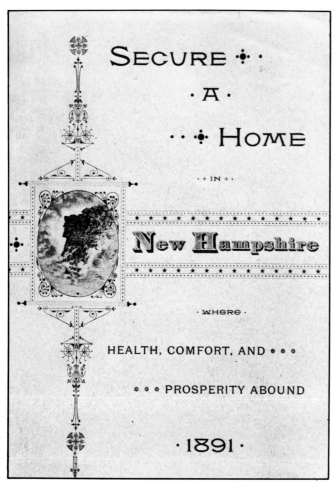

Title page of a state publication advertising farms and homes for sale in New Hampshire. Courtesy of New Hampshire Historical Society

Conway included a balloon ascension and parachute drop. The parachute became entangled with the balloon, causing the jumper to crash on the roof of a church. He was not injured, but he did not attempt the stunt again that day.

A major event of the 1899 season was the ascent of the first automobile up the old carriage road. The steam-powered vehicle of F. O. and F. E. Stanley was the first of many to successfully climb the mountain. It soon became a testing ground for early automobile designers. All hotels had boasted large livery stables, but the owners had to add auto garages and service areas after 1900. The arrival of automobiles brought great changes in the tourist business. The new tourists were not as wealthy as the former patrons of the grand hotels, but they traveled where they pleased, when they pleased. They wanted to get back to nature.

FRANK W. ROLLINS, President. ALLEN HOLLIS, Secretary, Concord, N. H. GEORGE T. CRUFT, Treasurer, 10 Tremont St., Boston. PHILIP W. AYRES, Forester.

PROGRAM
OF THE
SEVENTH ANNUAL MEETING
Society for Protection of New Hampshire Forests
WEDNESDAY, AUGUST 5, 1908
INTERVALE, N. H., INTERVALE HOUSE

10.30 A. M. Business Meeting. Election of Officers. Report of the Forester.

11.00 A. M. Forest Conditions and Needs in New Hampshire.

Taxation of Forest Lands.
MR. J. H. FOSTER of the United States Forest Service.

A State Forest Policy with especial reference to Protection from Fire.
MR. F. W. RANE, State Forester in Massachusetts.

2.30 P. M. The Proposed National Forest in the White Mountains.
An address by REV. EDWARD EVERETT HALE.

The Interest of Manufacturers in the White Mountain Forests.
MR. C. J. H. WOODBURY, Secretary of the National Cotton Manufacturers' Association.

The Influence of the Forest on the Development of Electricity.
MR. ALLEN HOLLIS, President Concord Electric Company.

4.30 P. M. Short Walking Excursion through the Cathedral Woods to Mount Surprise.

8.15 P. M. The Forests in the White Mountain Region, with lantern photographs.
PHILIP W. AYRES, Forester of the Society.

GOVERNOR ROLLINS WILL PRESIDE

Members of the State Forestry Commission and of the Forestry Committee of the State Federation of Women's Clubs will be present.

A CORDIAL INVITATION IS EXTENDED TO ALL WHO ARE INTERESTED

The back-to-nature movement began in the last quarter of the nineteenth century, when traveling Americans had an opportunity to see their great nation and to appreciate the beauty of the natural wilderness that was rapidly disappearing. This trend began when writers, artists, educators, and others became interested in spiritual regeneration. Nature writers became very popular, and the leading magazines like *Atlantic Monthly* and *Saturday Review* included nature articles for their readers. Books of photographs were published, revealing the beauties of natural areas like the White Mountains.

Summer camps were established so that urban youth could get back to nature and learn outdoor camping skills. Boy Scouts, Cub Scouts, Brownies, Girl Scouts, and Campfire Girls were just a few of the organizations that were formed to provide year-round contact with nature. Outing clubs kept adults involved in the outdoor

Senate bill proposing the purchase of land for the White Mountains National Forest. Courtesy of New Hampshire Historical Society

Program for the dedication of Franconia Notch Park on September 15, 1928. Courtesy of University of New Hampshire Special Collections

Society for Protection of New Hampshire Forests.

ADDRESSES

at the

DEDICATION of FRANCONIA NOTCH

September 15, 1928

movement as well. College outing clubs became very popular, and the Appalachian Mountain Club built its first hut in 1888.

The forest resource seemed inexhaustable until the 1870s, when naturalists, railroad interests, and hotel interests began to express concern about the condition of New Hampshire's forests. Joseph Walker fired the opening volley with a speech to the legislature in 1872. The *New England Homestead Magazine* joined the battle with a series of articles about the destruction of the forests.

In 1885 a permanent Forestry Commission issued a report of forest conditions in the state. Forest fires in Zealand alarmed the conservationists but it was Thomas Jefferson Coolidge, treasurer of the giant Amoskeag textile mills in Manchester, who forced the issue. Spring floods in 1895 and 1896 had caused the company to closed the mills and temporarily put six thousand people out of work. Coolidge blamed clear-cutting in the White Mountains for causing the floods, and other manufacturers along the waterways supported his claim.

So in 1901, industrialists, and some paper and lumber companies, joined forces with conservationists and tourist interests to form the Society for the Protection of New Hampshire's Forests. Led by Philip W. Ayers, the

society worked for the creation of a federal reservation in the White Mountains. It was a ten-year battle in Washington to get Congress to establish a national forest in New Hampshire. Congressmen from states without forests refused to support bills to spend millions of dollars for forest land, especially when the park would be entirely within the borders of New Hampshire. They recommended a state park, but there was no money for the state legislature to appropriate for such a purchase. Western states refused to support the proposal because their huge national parks had been carved from public forests and no land had to be purchased.

The issue finally gained congressional support in a bill to protect our rivers from flooding by creating forest reserves on the headwaters of the rivers and streams. The White Mountains were the source of the Saco, Merrimack, Androscoggin, and Connecticut rivers. The author of the bill was John W. Weeks, who was born and raised in Lancaster. He was very familiar with the river system in the mountains, and his bill provided for the purchase of a million acres of timberland, including an immense area along the Presidential Range. The acquisition of other tracts on the Sandwich and Franconia ranges and through the upper river valleys, enlarged the forest to cover more

THE FOUR RIVERS OF THE WHITE MOUNTAINS

The Androscoggin River originates in Lake Umbagog and, as it flows through New Hampshire, it is fed by Clear Stream, the Peabody, Swift, and Diamond rivers, and other smaller streams. The Androscoggin is approximately 60 miles long and drains an area of about 787 square miles.

The Connecticut River, the largest in New England, is about 450 miles long and drains about 3,600 square miles. Its principal tributaries in New Hampshire are Hall's Stream, Indian Stream, the Upper and Lower Ammonoosuc, Israel's River, John's River, the Mascomy, the Sugar, the Little Sugar, and the Ashuelot rivers. The Connecticut River empties into Long Island Sound.

The Merrimack River is formed by the junction of the Pemigewasset and Winni-pesaukee rivers. The headwaters of the Pemigewasset are in the White Mountains and the Franconia Range. The larger tributaries are the Baker's, Mad, Newfound, Squam, and Smith's rivers. The Pemigewasset River drains an area of approximately 1,000 square miles. The Winnipesaukee River is the outlet of Lake Winnipesaukee and it drains nearly 562 square miles. Below the junction of these two rivers, the Merrimack is fed by the Contoocook, the Soucook, the Turkey, the Piscataquog, the Souhegan, and the Nashua rivers. In New Hampshire, the Merrimack drains about 3,582 square miles.

The fourth major river is the Saco, which has three of its sources in the White Mountains. It flows 160 miles and is fed by the Swift and Ossipee rivers.

The four major rivers of the White Mountains and the streams that flow into them. Illustration by Ron White

Prospective fishermen waiting at the boat landing in Franconia Notch. Courtesy of New Hampshire Historical Society

than a thousand square miles.

Franconia Notch was saved when the state appropriation of two hundred thousand dollars was matched by the Society for the Protection of New Hampshire Forests, which raised its share from fifteen thousand donors. Conservationists also purchased other threatened areas, such as Lost River.

The new program did eventually lead to improved flood control, reduced soil erosion and expanded use of hydro power. The danger from forest fires was decreased and the state developed a fire service that was rated as one of the best in the country. The Timerland Owners

Association, organized by Rob Brown of the Berlin Company, hired fire patrols, trained fire crews, introduced safety equipment, and established fire lookout stations on the mountaintops. The State Forestry Service established a system of county and town fire wardens, trained volunteer crews, established twenty-eight fire towers, opened access roads, and built dams on streams to create water reservoirs.

State laws were passed to require the use of spark arresters by railroads and sawmills. Smoking was restricted in lumber camps, and outdoor burning was strictly regulated. The woods were closed to climbers, campers, and

Entrance to the Judgment Hall of Pluto at Lost River. A post card view. From the author's collection

hunters when conditions became dangerously dry and there was great potential for forest fires.

There was little that anyone could do to protect the forests from the terrible damage caused by the hurricane of 1938. The area had experienced a week of steady rains, bringing the rivers close to flood stage and softening the forest floors. The storm came on September 21, while hardwoods were still heavy with foliage. Thousands of trees fell on power lines and telephone lines. Roads were blocked by large trees and floods were fed by raging mountain streams. Crawford and Franconia notches were blocked by windfalls, and seven hundred miles of trails were closed. In the White Mountains National Forest, an estimated 175,000,000 feet of timber was down. Millions of feet of hurricane timber went to the mills in Berlin, which had become the largest pulp and paper center in the region. The timber market was flooded and many families had to take heavy losses on their most valuable asset and traditional source of winter work. Their wood lots were destroyed just before the war, when lumber prices soared to unheard-of levels.

5
MOUNTAIN ADVENTURES

It was nearly two hundred years after Darby Field's ascent of Mount Washington in 1642 before any other great mountain in the world was scaled. By the time the Matterhorn was conquered in 1865, horseback riding to the summit of Mountain Washington had become a popular adventure. The mountain was always a challenge for hikers even though the weather could range from a gorgeous summer day in the valley to a blinding ice storm on the peak. Mount Washington weather is given to sudden changes and those that hike or climb must be prepared for sudden blizzards and extreme drops in temperature. There are many stories of unprepared or poorly equipped climbers who suffered terribly because they underestimated the mountain.

The first recorded death on Mount Washington was that of twenty-nine-year-old Frederick Strickland on October 19, 1849. Strickland ignored his guide's advice to abandon a climb in deep snow. He went on alone, apparently fell into a pool of water, removed his frozen garments, and died from exposure close to his destination.

Lizzie C. Bourne of Kennebunk, Maine, is one of the best-known victims of the mountain. Four years after Strickland's death, Lizzie left the Glen House accompanied by her uncle George and his daughter Lucy. They left at two in the afternoon and walked up the carriage road as far as it had been completed at that time. They left the Halfway House at four, with the intention of following the path to the summit, where they would spend the night. They were less than two miles from the summit

From a B. W. Kilburn stereograph of the Glen House stage on the summit of Mount Washington. From the author's collection

A climber ascending Mount Washington in winter. From a Kilburn Brothers stereograph. From the author's collection

Halfway house on the Carriage Road to Mount Washington. From a Kilburn Brothers stereograph. From the author's collection

when darkness came and a high wind made progress difficult. A cloud hid the Summit House and the hikers had no idea they were so close to the top. Mr. Bourne made a crude stone shelter where they decided to remain until dawn. Early in the evening, twenty-three-year-old Lizzie died from heart failure only a short distance from shelter. The monument marking the location of this unfortunate event is near the railroad track, so the facts surrounding her death are well known.

A young Englishman perished the following year when he tried to climb the mountain alone. Another victim was elderly Benjamin Chandler, who left from the Glen and wandered from the trail. An extensive search was unsuccessful. A year later, his remains were found about a half-mile east of the summit. Another lone climber, Harry W. Hunter, perished about a half-mile from the summit near the Crawford Bridle Path. Six years later, his remains, partially hidden under an overhanging rock, were found by three young climbers. It was assumed that he crawled under the rock for shelter and died of exposure or heart failure. On August 24, 1890, Ewald Weiss left the Summit House on an unaccompanied trip to the summit of Mount Adams. He was never seen again. A watch, identified as belonging to Weiss, was discovered a year later on the eastern face of Mount John Quincy Adams. The search then shifted to that region, but his remains were never found.

A lithograph of Travelers in a Storm on Mount Washington, *by W. H. Gibson for* Drake's Heart of the White Mountains, *circa 1882.*

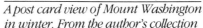

A post card view of Mount Washington in winter. From the author's collection

Mount Adams looms in the background as a White Mountain coach approaches a farmhouse. Courtesy of New Hampshire Historical Society

The ordeal of Dr. B. L. Ball, an extensive traveler and experienced climber, is one of the great mountain tales. The adventurous doctor had delayed several trips to Mount Washington and finally decided to make the trip in late October 1885. He took a train from Portland to Gorham in a heavy rainstorm and rode from the station to the Glen House on horseback. There was dense fog when he arrived and he decided to return. However, Mr. Thompson, the landlord, caused him to reconsider when he told him about the carriage road (then under construction), the Camp House, the Ledge and the bridle path to the summit. Protected by his umbrella, Dr. Ball determined to walk up the carriage road in spite of the heavy rain. It took him two hours to reach the Ledge, which he climbed without much difficulty. He continued in the freezing rain but had to return to the Camp House, where he spent the night with three other men.

There was a light rain falling in the morning. He ignored the warnings of his companions and continued his climb to the summit. Ball soon became exhausted from breaking through the snow crust, the air grew very cold, and the rain changed to sleet. The trail was difficult to follow, and he frequently wandered off course. He

EDGAR WELCH OF HIRAM, MAINE

During the period from 1900 to 1907, Edgar Welch came from Hiram, Maine, to make the run down the carriage road. Welch, who was over six feet tall, always came dressed in an old black suit, a black and white striped shirt, and a tall beaver hat from an earlier period. He usually spent several hours on the mountain, "training" in the back room, or bar, of the Summit House. After an extended warm-up on the platform in front of the Summit House, Welch would take off down the road with his arms flailing and the beaver hat perched securely on his head. At the age of fifty-one, he made the run in approximately forty-five minutes. This record has been broken by many runners, but none of them was wearing a beaver hat!

Edgar Welch starting his annual run down Mount Washington wearing his famous beaver hat. Circa 1900.

pushed himself to reach the summit where there would be food and shelter, but the storm grew more violent and he was unable to locate the buildings. The misguided adventurer decided to retrace his steps back down the mountain but the blowing snow had covered his tracks. A row of surveyor's stakes marked the proposed route of the carriage road and he followed them to the timberline, where they ended. Night was coming on and it was obvious that he would have to find shelter if he were going to survive.

Finding a crevasse between a rock and low patch of furze, Dr. Ball covered the opening with his umbrella and fastened it to a tough root. He piled bushes on top of the umbrella and used pieces of snow crust to cover the sides. It was too wet and windy to start a fire but he passed the night safely in the small shelter. His greatest challenge was to remain awake because even a few minutes' sleep could have been fatal. He shifted positions frequently while the storm roared around his fragile shelter.

At dawn on the next day he discovered that the snow had stopped but the windy mountainside was enveloped in clouds. He began to circle the mountain looking for evidence of a path. The crusty snow was eight or ten inches deep and there were many obstacles. After four hours of unsuccessful searching, Ball decided to return to his shelter. Upon his return, the clouds cleared away and two men appeared on a nearby bluff. They were guides who were part of a search party, but he was unable to attract their attention. The searchers had followed his

tracks to within a half-mile of his shelter, but left without finding him. Dr. Ball was forced to return to the crude shelter and spend another night struggling to keep awake while the storm threatened to destroy his cover.

The following morning was clear and Ball could see a building several miles away in a valley on the other side of a large forest. Ball decided to circle the mountain in the opposite direction from the previous day and look for a trail. At mid-day, he came upon a search party that had been following his tracks. They assisted him to the path which led to the Camp House, where he received treatment for his frozen feet. A horse carried him to the new road where he was met by a carriage sent to "pick up his body." It took Dr. Ball three months to recover from his ordeal, which provided material for a book called *Three Days on the White Mountains, being the Perilous Adventure of Dr. B. L. Ball on Mount Washington, during October 25, 26, 27, 1885, written by Himself—A Thrilling Narrative.*

Natural disasters, like the Willey landslide in 1826, are not uncommon occurrences in the mountains. On October 4, 1869, exceptionally heavy rains caused an avalanche on Carter Dome which stripped the mountain to its bed ledges for nearly a mile on the north and west slopes. Mr. Thompson, proprietor of the Glen House perished in the torrent of water and debris that was pushed down the Peabody River. A slide of Tripyramid, a triple-crown mountain in the Waterville region denuded a two-and-one-half-mile strip which was more than one thousand feet wide at the lower end. Another slide on

110

FABULOUS "FEETS"

Nathaniel Perkins, of Jefferson, ran one mile down the Glen path from the top of Mount Washington, on a bet of sixty dollars. He bet that the feat could be accomplished in eight minutes. His actual time was six minutes and fifty-seven seconds, in August 1853.

Ms. Branch won a bet of one thousand dollars when she walked from Glen to Tip-Top and back and danced at the Glen in the evening. The 230-pound woman was also the heaviest lady to visit Tip-Top as of July 25, 1855.

A. S. Walker of Boston walked up from the Glen to the top of Mount Washington, barefooted, July 26, 1855.

John Irving of New York walked from the Glen to the top of Mount Washington in an hour and fifty-seven minutes, August 1855.

Miss Prentiss of Paris, Maine, walked from the Glen to the top of Mount Washington, in a snowstorm, without a guide, August 22, 1856.

George N. Dana of Boston counted his steps from the Glen to the top of Mount Washington, August 2, 1857. The number of steps was 16,925.

"Fabulous Feets."
Illustration by Ron White

Tourists in the Flume in the 1880s.
Courtesy of New Hampshire Historical
Society

From a stereograph by B. W. Kilburn
showing the boulder firmly lodged in the
Flume. From the author's collection

Joe Dodge dressed for work. Courtesy of Mount Washington Observatory Collection

Carter's Notch from Jackson, New Hampshire. Courtesy of University of New Hampshire Special Collections

Tripyramid in 1885 was even more destructive, but no lives were lost. The huge boulder suspended between the narrow walls in the upper part of the Flume was swept away by an avalanche on June 20, 1883. The loss was offset by the addition of two waterfalls. The "Stanley Slide" occurred on Cherry Mountain on July 10, 1885. A two-mile track of devastation deposited broken trees, mud, rocks, and earth on the farm of Oscar Stanley. It destroyed his house, killed several cattle, and fatally injured a farmhand.

The Appalachian Mountain Club was founded in 1876 and has done more than any other organization to support safe hiking across the big range. The club built a hut between Mount Madison and Mount Adams, a hut in nearby Carter Notch, and a shelter, then a hut, at Lakes of the Clouds.

In 1920 the AMC authorized the construction of two log cabins in Pinkham Notch, and in 1922, Joe Dodge,

then twenty-two years old, was hired as summer manager of the little camp. Joe loved the wilderness and he came back each summer. In 1926 managing the camp became his full-time job. An ever-increasing stream of hikers added to his responsibilities. He developed an elaborate short-wave station to connect the camp with the Harvard College weather station on Blue Hill in Massachusetts. The link was through the Mount Washington Observatory on the summit of Mount Washington. Joe Dodge, through his direct rescue efforts and the use of ham radio, assisted with the rescue of many injured or lost hikers. He made the mountains a safer place for everyone.

Norman Libby of Bridgeton, Maine, was the first person to ski down Mount Washington when he made the trip on February 16, 1905. Mr. Libby, who was the assistant editor of *Among the Clouds*, returned in 1907 and made the four-mile run down the carriage road, from the

Skiers were challenged by the mere presence of Mount Washington. Willie Hastings was one of the early skiers to test the mountain. Courtesy of Mount Washington Observatory Collection

Skiing down the headwall at Tuckerman's Ravine. Mount Washington Observatory Staff Photo

Halfway House to the Glen House, in twenty minutes.

The first crude, homemade skis had appeared at Dartmouth College in the 1890s, and the Dartmouth Outing Club was formed in 1910. Its first president was Fred Harris, an accomplished ski runner and jumper. As skiing grew more popular, the D.O.C. members were challenged by the presence of Mount Washington. Although many enthusiasts had skied down the mountain, in March 1913, three members of the P.O.A. were the first from any club to make the *ascent* on skis.

Charles A. Proctor, a professor of physics at Dartmouth, was largely responsible for the establishment of the Eastern Intercollegiate Ski Union, which included Dartmouth, New Hampshire College, and McGill University. This evolved from the Dartmouth Winter Carnival, which began in 1911 and stimulated great interest in winter sports among the northern colleges. Proctor's son Charles N., and John P. Carleton were the first to ski the

Tuckerman headwall, a sheer drop of one thousand feet into the bowl below. They made the dangerous run on April 11, 1931.

Through the hard work and foresight of entrepreneurs, especially in the Jackson/Conway area, skiing was becoming popular with winter sports fans, and snow trains brought thousands of enthusiasts to the mountains each weekend. Facilities were strained to acommodate the weekend crowds, but they were deserted during the week. On March 20, 1932, the Nansen Ski Club of Berlin, the Glen House, and Joe Dodge sponsored the Mount Washington Spring Snow Fest. They conducted a series of races and jumping events for girls, boys, and senior skiers. The featured event was an eight-mile race down the carriage road, sanctioned by the Eastern Amateur Ski Association, which attracted the top Olympic and college stars.

A seventy-mile-an-hour gale threatened to cancel the race but five of the skiers were not turned away by the strong winds. Traveling at blinding speed, with the gale at their backs, the skiers completed the first race from the summit to the Glen House in slightly over twelve minutes. The winner was Edward J. Blood of the University of New Hampshire, who was only twenty-five seconds ahead of the last man to cross the finish line.

The first ski race from the summit down over the Tuckerman headwall was held on April 16, 1933. Billed as the first American Inferno, the course was so hazardous that many considered the race to be suicidal. Fourteen racers entered and the race took place on wet snow in driving rain. Hollis Phillips, the only racer to come down on his feet, won in a time of approximately seventeen minutes. In the April 1939 race, Toni Matt schussed the headwall at sixty miles an hour to the amazement of four thousand spectators. His time of 6:29.4 was a full minute faster than that of the second-place finisher.

Two-boys fishing from a log in Cole Pond in the late 1800s. Courtesy of New Hampshire Historical Society

6

POETS, WRITERS AND PAINTERS

The White Mountains, an area of great scenic beauty and rugged wilderness, attracted adventurers with a great variety of interests. Scientists in search of botanical and geologic specimens were among the early visitors. They made sketches of the landscape, plant life, and other natural features. Artists Thomas Cole and Henry Cheever Pratt came to the White Mountains in 1827 and 1828. They both returned with sketchbooks and diaries. Cole produced numerous paintings from his sketches. In the paintings he manipulated the elements to produce an idealized image of the mountain scenery.

Alvan Fisher came in 1834 and painted the south end of the notch showing the Willey house overwhelmed by the magnificent mountains. Cole returned in the fall of 1839 and his painting of the notch reflected the presence of the Crawford family and the changes that they had introduced.

Lucy Crawford, wife of Ethan Allen Crawford, published *The History of the White Mountains from the First Settlement of the Upper Coos and Pequaket* in 1845-46. It

The White Mountains of New Hampshire, *engraved by Fenner, Sears & Company, after a painting by Thomas Cole. Courtesy of New Hampshire Historical Society*

FRANKLIN LEAVITT, WHITE MOUNTAIN POET

Franklin Leavitt was a well-known White Mountain guide who was often employed by the Crawford family. Leavitt drew primitive maps of the White Mountains which he printed and sold to tourists.

He also wrote verse which he printed for sale to the tourists. Leavitt's *Poems of the White Mountains,* containing many of these verses, was published by the author. He wrote the following verse about the Willey slide:

Detail from a Frank Leavitt map that was printed in 1878. Courtesy of New Hampshire Historical Society

> Eighteen hundred and twenty-six
>   The Willey mountain down
>   did slip.
> It missed the house and hit the barn;
>   If they'd all staid in they'd met
>   no harm.
> It being in the dark of night
>   The Willey family took a fright,
> And out of the house they all did run
>   And on to them the mountains
>   come.
>
> It buried them all up so deep
>   They did not find them for
>   three weeks,
> And three of them were never found
>   They were buried there so deep
>   in the ground.

A page of Frank Leavitt's poems. Courtesy of New Hampshire Historical Society

The Lower Cascade near Crawford Notch. From an 1848 lithograph by Isaac Sprague for William Oakes' Scenery of the White Mountains.

Profile Mountain in Franconia Notch. From an 1848 lithograph by Isaac Sprague for William Oakes' Scenery of the White Mountains.

E. A. CRAWFORD AND THE BEARS

The first bear kept at the White Mountains to entertain travelers was captured by Ethan Allen Crawford in 1829, while returning from a trip up the mountain with two young men. A small bear crossed their path and they chased him up a tree. Ethan went up the tree and managed to tie his mouth with a handkerchief. He carried the bear home on his back. The bear was kept strapped to a pole where he was a great curiosity.

At another time, Ethan caught a wild buck in a snare. The deer was too heavy to carry, so he made a halter and managed to lead the animal home through the wilderness. Earlier he had carried a large deer home on his back only to have it die from its injuries.

A portrait of Benjamin Champney at work in his studio in 1900. Courtesy of University of New Hampshire Special Collections

A wide-angle view of Chapney's North Conway studio. Courtesy of University of New Hampshire Special Collections

Champney's charcoal of Crystal Falls in Pinkham Notch from B. J. Willey's Incidents in White Mountain History. *Courtesy of University of New Hampshire Special Collections*

was the simple story of Ethan Crawford's life told in the picturesque language of his heroic and faithful wife.

The distinguished New England botanist William Oakes came each season to add to his collection of White Mountains plants. In 1848 he published his *Scenery of White Mountains*, a folio with sixteen plates, the first illustrations of real consequence from the mountain region. In 1853 Professor George P. Bond of the Harvard Observatory published the first authentic sketch map of the White Mountains with a table of heights, bearings, and distances. His first copy, unfortunately, mislabeled two of the Presidential peaks. The map included five lithographs from drawings by Benjamin Champney.

Dr. Charles Jackson's *Final Report*, issued in 1844, was the first geological survey of New Hampshire. It contained four hundred pages of geological, mineralogical, and agricultural information and identified many minerals and mineral locations which were previously unknown. His discovery of tin was considered to be particularly significant. He was a member of Abel Crawford's party, which was the first to reach the summit of Mount Washington on horseback in 1840. President Hitchcock of Amherst College published a series of illuminating articles on the geology and scenery of the White Mountains in the *Boston Recorder*. Arnold Guyot was engaged

in a study of the physical configuration of the Appalachian Mountain system.

The first serious attempt to write the history of this region was by Rev. Benjamin G. Willey, the brother of Samuel Willey, who perished with his family in the great slide of 1826. His book, *Incidents in White Mountain History*, which is also a guide to the area, contains one of the best accounts of the disaster, and treats the stories of early settlement and Indian traditions as well. Sketches by Mr. Champney make the book even more interesting. John H. Spaulding, a keeper of the summit houses, published a collection of anecdotes and legends called *Historical Relics of the White Mountains*, which is much less trustworthy and is not to be compared with Willey's effort. It was during this period that Thomas W. Parsons wrote the stirring commemorative ballad "The Willey House," inspired by the destruction of the Willey family.

The first European images of the White Mountains appeared in John Hinton's Illustrated *History and Topography of the United States of America*, published in London in 1831. Three of the engravings were after Thomas Cole's paintings including *The Storm Near Mount Washington*. Nathaniel P. Willis's *American Scenery*, published in London in 1838-39, was decorated with engravings after drawings made by British illustrator

NATHANIEL HAWTHORNE VISITS ETHAN CRAWFORD

Nathaniel Hawthorne described his visit to Ethan Allen Crawford's mountain inn in his book *Mosses From An Old Manse*. In a sketch titled "Our Evening Party Among the Mountains," he wrote:

> Ethan Crawford's guests were of such a motley description as to form quite a picturesque group, seldom seen together except at some place like this, at once the pleasure house of fashionable tourists and the homely inn of country travelers. Among the company at the door were the mineralogist and the owner of the golden opera glass whom we had encountered in the Notch; two Georgia gentlemen, who had chilled their southern blood that morning on top of Mount Washington; a physician and his wife from Conway; a trader of Burlington and an old squire of the Green Mountains; and two young married couples, all the way from Massachusetts, on the matrimonial jaunt. Besides these strangers, the rugged county of Coos, in which we were, was represented by a half dozen woodcutters, who had slain a bear in the forest and smitten off his paw.

Hawthorne contemplated returning in "sleighing time" to study the characters who traveled through the notch by the hundreds on their way to Portland. He planned to share their evening meals, participate in their evening merriment, and sleep with them at night, every bed having three occupants, and the parlor, barroom, and kitchen being "strewn with slumberers around the fire." He felt there would be no better school for studying the yeomen of New England than Crawford's Inn in December.

Nathaniel Hawthorne. Courtesy of University of New Hampshire Media Services

William H. Bartlett, who had visited the United States in 1836. This book featured eleven views of New Hampshire and the White Mountains, indicating the popularity of the region with foreign travelers.

Nathaniel Hawthorne came through the notch in 1832. He stopped with Ethan Allen Crawford at the Giant's Grave and climbed to the summit of Mount Washington. His visit was brief, but it provided material for *The Great Stone Face, The Ambitious Guest*, and *The Great Carbuncle.* John Greenleaf Whittier has sometimes been called the poet of the hills. He was a frequent visitor to the lakes and mountains about which he wrote "The

Bridal of Pennacook," the ballad of "Mary Garvin," and "The Hilltop."

Whittier's first poem about the region was called "The White Mountains" and was in his first book, an 1831 publication, *Legends of New England in Prose and Verse*. The title of the poem was changed to "Mount Agiochook" in the author's complete works. Early in the 1840s, Whittier made a journey through the heart of the notch by stagecoach and ascended Mount Washington. The prologue to "The Bridal of Pennacook," published in 1844, opened with a glorified itinerary of that experience. In 1856 he published the poem "Mary Garvin," which deals

John Greenleaf Whittier. Courtesy of University of New Hampshire Media Services

The Whittier Covered Bridge. 1985 lithograph by Ron White

descriptively with the mouth of the Saco River. In 1865 the poet boarded at Selden Willey's farm, where his friends James and Annie Field were staying. Here his poem "Franconia from the Pemigewasset" was expanded from an earlier version.

The success of "Snow-Bound" made Whittier financially independent. In the summer of 1867, he stayed at the Bearcamp River House in West Ossipee. Ames Tavern, later called Bank's Hotel, had formerly been on this site and provided accommodations for Starr King and artists George Inness, George L. Brown, and Benjamin Champney. In such surroundings Whittier wrote "Among the Hills," a companion piece to "Snow-Bound." Whittier spent several summers and autumns at the Bearcamp River House. The hotel was sometimes filled with his friends and relatives, and such reunions gave him great pleasure. Other poems written to celebrate the beauties of the region include, "Sunset on the Bearcamp" and "Voyage of the Jettie." The hotel burned in 1881 and Whittier spent several weeks that summer at Intervale with his cousins, Joseph and Gertrude Cartland. He was with them each summer for the remaining twelve years of his life.

Early view of Cathedral Woods in North Conway, New Hampshire. Courtesy of New Hampshire Historical Society

An artist and a peddler meet on a White Mountain road. From the White Mountain Echo, *1883-84. Courtesy of University of New Hampshire Special Collections*

The Intervale House, circa 1890. Courtesy of Ossipee Historical Society

TRIAL BY FIRE

In the Crawford Notch area, Horace Fabyan expanded Ethan Allen Crawford's old hotel, the Mount Washington House. In the period from 1845 to 1846, he added a three-story, 140-foot building. In 1848 he started construction of a one hundred-bed wing which was completed in 1850. Two years later, he was able to advertize that "there were ample outhouses adjoining." The entire complex was destroyed by fire in the spring of 1853. There was a dispute over who owned the land, and the hotel was not rebuilt for nearly ten years.

Thomas J. Crawford had expanded the Notch House but developed plans for another hotel on the opposite side of the road. Construction began in 1850s, but Crawford had financial problems and sold out to Colonel J. L. Gibb who opened the new hotel, called the Crawford House, in 1851. In 1854, the Notch House burned to the ground.

With no competition from the Mount Washington House and the Notch House, the Crawford House dining room capacity was expanded to seat three hundred people. The hotel was consumed by fire on April 31, 1859, but the owners were determined to rebuild and opened in a new building before July 1, 1860.

The White Mountain House was the only one in the Crawford Notch area that survived the fires of the 1850s. At that time it was operated by Col. John White.

The Gate to Crawford Notch showing Thomas J. Crawford's Notch House. From an 1848 lithograph by Isaac Sprague for William Oakes' Scenery of the White Mountains

An attempt was made to save the Crawford House from demolition but fund-raising attempts were unsuccessful. Source unknown

Old Crawford House Will Be Demolished

TWIN MOUNTAIN, N.H. (AP) — Negotiations have broken down try to postpone the liquidation of the history Crawford House here and an auction of the hotel's contents was to begin today.

George McAvoy, one of the owners of the 165-room hotel, said Sunday that he regretted having to auction off the hotel, but that its operation was no longer economically feasible.

McAvoy, who is state director of comprehensive planning and has considerable holdings in the White Mountains, said those attempting to intervene in the auction were "totally unrealistic" in their approach to the problem.

A number of groups, including the New Hampshire Historical Society and the Appalachian Mountain Club, had sought to put off the auction for 90 days. Society officials said more than $8,000 had been pledged to the cause.

The hotel was a landmark in the White Mountains. But it had become a problem for its owners. McAvoy said nearly a dozen persons had been caught breaking into the property in the past month.

The contents of the hotel are to be auctioned off over three or four days this week. Afterward the building was scheduled to be torn down.

McAvoy announced earlier this month that it was no longer feasible for him and the other owners to operate the hotel.

He said various historical groups had sought to put off the auction for three months. He said the postponment would cost him $2,500 a month insurance and would leave him with having to break an agreement with the auctioneer.

John Page, director of the New Hampshire Historical Society, said last week pledges of $8,000 had been received and another $5,000 might be sufficient to put of the auction. But negotiations broke down Saturday night.

Others involved in the attempted intervention were the New Hampshire Charitable Fund, the Society for the Protection of New Hampshire Forests, and the Nature Conservancy, as well as several individuals.

The hotel was built 117 years ago. During the weekend, hundreds of people visited the hotel. A number of the older visitors said they had once worked there when

Crawford House. Courtesy of Ossipee Historical Society

An artist sketching at The Emerald Pool. *An original stereograph by J. Soule & Company. Courtesy of New Hampshire Historical Society*

Lucy Larcom, a lifelong friend of Whittier, became a regular visitor to the region in the 1860s. She summered in Campton, Ossipee, Sandwich, Berlin Falls, Bethlehem, Mount Moosilauke, and Center Harbor. She wrote many beautiful poems on these trips, including "Up the Androscoggin," "Asleep on the Summit," "Clouds on Whiteface," "Hills in the Mist," "My Mountain," and many others. "Mountaineer's Prayer" was written on the summit of Moosilauke on September 7, 1892, the day after Whittier's death. She passed away in April 1893, a victim of heart disease.

The flow of artists and tourists was increased by the completion of the Atlantic & St. Lawrence Railroad's route through Gorham in 1851 and the Boston, Concord & Montreal Railroad to Littleton in 1853. Existing hotels were expanded but new ones had to be built. These included the Crawford House and Alpine House in 1851, the Glen House in 1852, and the Profile House in 1853. The work of the artists attracted tourists which, in turn, attracted more artists. One early gathering spot for artists

was at Thompson's Tavern (later the Kearsarge House) in North Conway. Benjamin Champney and John F. Kensett stayed at the tavern during the summer of 1850, and by 1853 approximately forty artists were summering in North Conway. Several of the most influential Hudson River School painters were headquartered in North Conway, including Kensett, Jasper Cropsey, Asher B. Durand, and Albert Bierstadt.

Benjamin Champney, who had been studying art in Europe, attracted other artists to the area and began to increase the interest in cultural affairs on the eastern slopes of Mount Washington. The White Mountain School of Art developed because a group of artists working with related subjects followed a similar style, shared ideas about their work, and exhibited in the same institutions. The White Mountain painters continued to show the influence of the Hudson River School, a style that stressed the picturesque. Their work was geared to the taste and pocketbooks of the middle class.

While some of the White Mountain School artists

Guests gather on the lawn of the Kearsarge House in North Conway, New Hampshire, in an original stereograph by N. W. Pease. Courtesy of New Hampshire Historical Society

Cover of Thomas Starr King's popular book on the White Mountains. Courtesy of University of New Hampshire Special Collections

were summer residents, many of them remained in the area through the long winters. The school survived for an extended period because artists like Champney had a large number of pupils who worked under his guidance and produced many paintings in the tradition of the White Mountain School.

The daguerreotype was the earliest form of photography in this country, and it is only natural that the first landscape photographers would have been attracted to the White Mountains. It is possible that the first landscape to be photographed in this country was Crawford Notch by Samuel Bemis in about 1840.

An idealized view of the region was perpetuated by a series of guidebooks, which made the area seem more accessible and exciting. Thomas Starr King's 1859 publication, *The White Hills: Their Legends, Landscape and Poetry*, directed visitors to perfect viewing spots with an intensity that was reinforced by poetry and illustrations. King lived for months in the mountains and he visited them during every season of the year. As a guidebook,

The White Hills delineates in detail every route into the region. As a topographical manual, it carefully describes the face of the country, including every striking view. Its rich descriptions of every variety of landscape can apply to all natural scenes.

Other artists who were painting and sketching in the White Mountains in the 1840s and 1850s were Chester Harding, who painted Abel Crawford in 1846, B. G. Stone, who painted the Crystal Cascade in 1851, and Samuel Colman, who produced the romantic ruins of *The Grand Gulf*, a painting that was admired by Thomas Starr King. It was about this time that Daniel Huntington painted *Chocorua Peak* and George L. Brown completed his well-known work *The Crown of New England*, which was painted from Martin's farm near the site of the Mount Adams House in Jefferson Highlands.

After the Civil War, rail lines met the needs of tourists by building spurs to the major hotels. The region became a place where Americans could go in comfort and experience one of the last wilderness areas of the country.

Crawford Notch and Mount Washington
    six hotels, 1,500 capacity
Bethlehem
    twenty-four hotels, 1,450 capacity
North Conway
    seventeen hotels, 1,070 capacity
Glen-Gorham
    four hotels, 700 capacity
Jefferson
    eleven hotels, 665 capacity
Franconia Notch
    two hotels, 540 capacity
Lancaster
    nine hotels, 400 capacity
Littleton
    nine hotels, 300 capacity
Jackson
    four hotels, 200 capacity

Noted visitors to White Mountain hotels in the 1870s included Horace Greeley, who visited in 1872 during his presidential campaign, President Rutherford B. Hayes, Vice-President William A. Wheeler, Cornelius Vanderbilt, Gen. Joseph Hooker, Cyrus W. Field, and John Greenleaf Whittier.

Illustrated ads for the Sinclair House, the Kearsarge House and Randlet's Hotel from the White Mountain Echo. *Courtesy of New Hampshire Historical Society*

Advertisements for the Goodnow House and Franconia House from an 1884 issue of Among the Clouds. *Courtesy of New Hampshire Historical Society*

Rates for Season: At hotel, $14 per week and upward; at cottage, $9 per week and upward. Private cottages, $80 to $100 per month; with table board at hotel, $9 per week.

O. D. SEAVEY,
(OF HOTEL BRUNSWICK, BOSTON.)

SINCLAIR HOUSE

BETHLEHEM, N.H.

DURGIN & FOX
PROPRIETORS

RANLET'S
American and European Hotel
BETHLEHEM.

RANLET'S
Cafe and Ice Cream Parlor
Adjoins the Hotel.
ALL ORDERS PROMPTLY ATTENDED

KIARSARGE HOUSE,
NORTH CONWAY.

One of the largest houses on the line of the Portland & Ogdensburg and Eastern Railroad.
Spacious halls, corridors and parlors.
Table unexcelled by any house in the Mountains.
Bath-rooms and every accommodation pertaining to a first-class hotel.

TERMS: $3 and $3.50 a Day to Transients. Special Rates persons desiring to remain part or all of the Season.

S. W. and S. D. THOMPSON, Managers.

BATH HOTEL,
37, 39 & 41, West 26th Street, New York City,
NEAR FIFTH AVENUE AND MADISON PARK.

FRANCONIA.

GOODNOW HOUSE,
FRANCONIA.

This well-known house is open for the Season.
Accommodation and prices as usual.
Table supplied from farm near the house.
The highest elevation in Franconia.

E. H. GOODNOW, Proprietor.

FRANCONIA HOUSE,
NEAR PROFILE HOUSE, FRANCONIA, N. H.

This house is located on high ground, and commands an extensive view of the Mountains and surrounding country.
LARGE FARM AND GOOD LIVERY STABLE
Connected.
Prices from $7 to $9 per Week. Send for Circular.

H. W. PRIEST, Proprietor.

Hotels supp notice.

HOWAR

For Sale at and the Nove the Mountains

Manufacture

CONVENTION SEASON

During the last two decades of the nineteenth century, White Mountain hotels began to cater to large convention groups. Many of the hotels were large enough to house the entire meeting under one roof, and the Bethlehem area could provide convention facilities for over one thousand people. For example, in 1884, five hundred members of the Brotherhood of Locomotive Engineers met at Fabyans, and in 1889, over one thousand members of the American Institute of Instruction held

their annual convention in Bethlehem. Other organizations that held their conventions in the White Mountains were the Christian Endeavorers, the Knights Templar, the International Association of Ticket Agents, the Independent Order of Railway Conductors, the American Association for the Advancement of Science, the Congress of Women's Clubs of New Hampshire, and the Appalachian Mountain Club.

In addition, September and October

became popular times for excursion parties or tours to be organized by travel agencies such as Raymond, Prescott, Camp, and Pinkham. These excursionists sometimes spent as little as sixty-five dollars for a fourteen-day vacation which included room, board, and transportation. The income generated by such large numbers of vacationers— was considerable and made it worthwhile for the owners to keep the hotels open in the fall.

Automobiles are the center of attention by guests of the Sinclair Hotel in Bethlehem, New Hampshire. From the author's collection

Trains at the railroad station in front of Fabyan's Hotel. From the author's collection

These guests look slightly uncomfortable climbing Mount Willard on Crawford House burros. From the author's collection

An original stereograph of tourists at the Mount Kearsarge summit house in the late 1800s. Courtesy of New Hampshire Historical Society

Tourism brought more revenue to towns like North Conway, Bethlehem, and Gorham than could be earned from agriculture or manufacturing. Existing hotels were enlarged and new ones were built, introducing such commodities as gas lights, electric lights, private toilets, and elevators. Hotels provided elaborate meals and amused guests with brass bands and coaching parades. But the growing tourist industry needed more sophisticated publicity. Newspapers, including *The White Mountain Echo and Tourist Register* and *Among the Clouds*, were published for distribution to summer residents. Maps and guidebooks were produced in large quantities.

Artists like Champney, Shapleigh, and Shattuck, now regular summer residents, produced a great number of paintings to meet the demands of the tourists. These artists began to base their work on the more traditonal

views of the area because they were more commercially viable. The growing demand for dramatic but accurate pictures led to an expansion of photography. The art community rejected photography as essentially mechanical and many of the early photographers were challenged to give their work the same qualities as paintings. So photographers filled the demand for inexpensive images to serve as memories of favorite places, but fortunately they posed no threat to the artists. By 1870 nearly every White Mountain resort community had a resident photographer. Benjamin and Edward Kilburn opened a studio in Littleton just after the Civil War. They eventually dominated the industry, producing 300,000 stereographs annually during the 1890s. Of course, town views and books illustrated with photographs assiduously avoided images of clear-cut forests, unkempt farms, wet tourists, or

A lithograph by Currier and Ives of Echo Lake from the popoular book by Thomas Starr King.

attacks by black flies and mosquitoes.

Currier and Ives, Louis Prang, and others published lithographs and nostalgic White Mountain scenes, and woodcuts in popular magazines provided a positive image of the region. Hundreds of artists flocked to the hotels and produced thousands of paintings. However, the region began to change, and so did the esthetics of the artists. Commercial development, the lumber industry, and the improvement in the highway system contributed to the commercial success of the region, but the artists were unable to adapt to the new conditions. Artists had been hired by the railroads and the hotels as an additional attraction to the area, but with the rise of the automobile and the decline of the railroads, and with vacationers looking for less expensive lodgings than the grand hotels offered, the tenor of the mountain resorts changed, and their patrons did not support the once-thriving artistic community.

A steam train crossing a trestle in Crawford Notch with Mount Webster in the background. From a stereograph by B. W. Kilburn. From the author's collection

A lithograph by Currier and Ives of the Falls of Ammonoosac. From Thomas Starr King's The White Hills: Their Legends, Landscape, and Poetry.

A post card view of Echo Lake in Franconia Notch. From the author's collection

ECHO LAKE, FRANCONIA NOTCH, WHITE MTS. N.H.

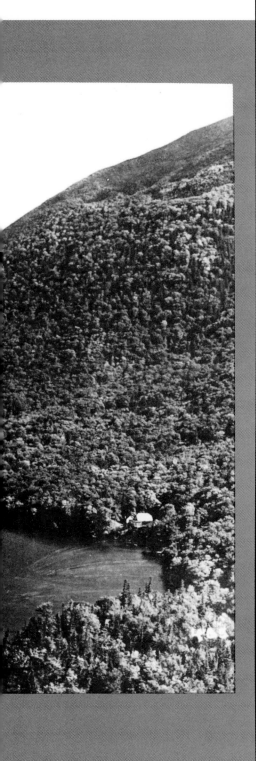

7

WHITE MOUNTAIN MAGIC

It took the Appalachian Mountin Club (AMC) seventy-seven years to build the system of eight huts which extends more than fifty miles along the mountain ridges of New Hampshire. The club built its first hut on Mount Madison in 1888, on a site donated by the Brown Lumber Company. This site was selected because it was near Randolph, a hiking center, and had an excellent source of spring water. Over the years, seven more huts were built from Lonesome Lake near Franconia Notch to Carter Notch near the Maine border. The system's headquarters at Pinkham Notch was expanded to hold ninety guests.

The first hut had no caretaker and soon was vandalized. Its wooden floor was burned for fuel and hikers had to sleep on earth or mud. It proved to be popular, in spite of its shortcomings, and a new room was added in 1906. The club hired a hutmaster, who made repairs, controlled vandals, sold supplies, provided blankets, and collected fees. Eventually the hutmaster prepared meals, which became very popular with the hikers, but required a crew to backpack tons of food and supplies into the mountain huts.

Success at Madison led to the construction of huts at Carter Notch in 1914 and Lake of the Clouds a year later.

A post card view of the hut on Mount Madison. The message said, "Tell grammy that I will write to her as soon as I have time." From the author's collection

The Lake of the Clouds on Mount Washington. From the author's collection

Mt. Liberty and the covered bridge are both snow covered in this scenic view of Franconia Notch. From the author's collection

The AMC built the Pinkham Notch camp just after World War I and hired Charles MacIntosh as supervisor of the four huts in 1919. He was replaced by Milton MacGregor, who served as manager until 1927. Joe Dodge was hired to operate the Pinkham facility which was opened year-round in 1926. Joe arrived during the controversy over the disposal of the Franconia Notch area, the home of the Old Man of the Mountain. The Flume and Profile hotels had burned in 1923 and the owners sold six thousand acres to timber investors. Conservationists, led by the AMC and the Society for the Protection of New Hampshire's Forests, raised enough money to match a state appropriation and purchase the area for public use.

The AMC hut system eventually became part of the Appalachian Trail being planned by Benton MacKaye. However, at that time Joe Dodge was working with a discontinuous collection of huts. When he retired in 1959, he had established a series of huts where hikers could find food and bedding, with each hut being a day's hike from the next. The huts were also educational centers with resident naturalists who led hikes and taught natural history.

The cog railway, which only ran three months each year and showed little, if any, profit, was owned by the Boston & Maine Railroad. Boston & Maine officials were frustrated with maintenance problems and the continuous search for operating personnel. In 1931, they delegated the responsibility of disposing of the cog railway to Laurence Whittemore, assistant to the B&M president. He tried to interest a group of White Mountain hotel men in assuming operation of the three-and-a-half-mile railroad but they were not prepared to take it on. At length, Whittemore arranged to sell the railroad to Henry M. Teague, an enthusiastic promoter who had never before been in the railroad business. He was broke, but they sold him the system for $100,000, all on a mortgage, and loaned him $10,000 for operating expenses.

The Rollins shelter at Lost River in the White Mountains. From the author's collection

A blazing fire welcomes visitors to the Rollins shelter at Lost River. From the author's collection

A scenic view of Mount Lafayette. From the author's collection

141

Colonel Henry N. Teague, who purchased the Mount Washington Cog Railway in 1931. Photo by Stanley Bauman; courtesy Mount Washington Observatory Collection

Henry Teague developed the Marshfield area at the foot of the railway. At its center was a log building which housed a restaurant and souvenir store. There was a large stone chimney with two fireplaces to warm chilled travelers when they came down off the mountain. There were also several cabins and a boardinghouse for railway employees. Other buildings housed the machine shop, train sheds and the electric power plant. The generation of electricity required 150 tons of coal each season. Teague installed a waterwheel, which was powered by Monroe Brook. The waterwheel ran a generator to power a water pump, which delivered ten gallons a minute to the Summit House through a two-inch pipe. It also provided electricity for all the restaurants, cabins, and machine shops at the base.

Teague increased the schedule of two trains each day to a train every hour. He introduced moonlight train rides, replaced old-time union help with college boys, put up roadside signs, distributed folders to hotel and cabin owners, and visited every convention within driving distance.

The volume of business increased five times. In his best season he carried thirty-five thousand passengers, compared to seven thousand in the best season under B&M management. In 1938 a new passenger car was built and all cars were enlarged to hold forty-eight instead of forty passengers. In 1941 turnouts were installed at the Base Station and the Waumbek Tank. A turnout was also installed at the Gulf Tank in the following year, and the cog railroad was no longer a one-way system. The turnout mechanism required eighteen different moves to operate, but it took less than five minutes for the shiftover and passing of two trains on a cog track.

The 1938 hurricane destroyed Jacob's Ladder and a half mile of trestle. The cost of reconstruction was $60,000, which Henry borrowed from his alma mater, Dartmouth College. Teague never married, and when he died in 1951, he left all his property to the college. This included a summit tract of fifty-nine acres with buildings thereon, the Mount Washington Cog Railway, and the

A post card view of the new Marshfield House, the cog railway, and Mount Washington. From the author's collection

Marshfield Base Station.

Arthur Teague, no relation, was Henry's longtime assistant. He became manager of the property on Henry's death and, in 1962, the college sold the railway and Marshfield base station to him. It retained the summit area until 1964, when it was sold to the state for public use. Arthur Teague continued to improve the cog railway system during the fifteen years of his ownership. He was assisted by his wife, Ellen Crawford Teague, a descendant of Abel and Ethan Allen Crawford. Ellen became president and treasurer of the Mount Washington Railway Company when Arthur died in 1967.

The state purchased fifty-nine acres on the summit from Dartmouth College for $150,000. In 1969 the legislature, which had long been concerned with the destiny of the mountaintop, established a committee to study the problem of renovating the buildings. Led by its chairman, Sherman Adams of Lincoln, the commission developed plans for a new Summit House to replace the 1915 structure. The fourth Summit House was semi-circular in

design and faced the northern Presidentials, a view for which Mount Washington is famous. The two-story building had entrances on the second floor because the lower floor hugged the ground to avoid the powerful winter storms and high winds that swirled around the peak.

The structure had twenty-two thousand feet of floor space for the railway's post office, a museum and lecture area, refreshment and restroom facilities for visitors, and emergency space for hikers. The unusual postal unit is "Mount Washington, N.H., 03589." Tens of thousands of greetings are mailed to all parts of the world from the tip of Mount Washington each year. The Mount Washington Observatory was housed at one end of the new building.

The new development also included the rebuilding of the Tip-Top House, the second structure built on the mountaintop in 1853. The state Division of Parks, in the Department of Resources and Economic Development, assumed responsibility for the building, which was placed on the National Register of Historic Places.

In 1880 a forty-foot-high wooden tower was built

Sherman Adams at the dedication of the fourth Summit House. Courtesy of Mount Washington Observatory Collection

The new Summit House with fuel storage tanks in the foreground. Mount Washington Observatory Staff Photo

A construction photograph of the fourth Summit House which has twenty-two thousand square feet of floor space, including the Observatory tower. Courtesy of Mount Washington Observatory Collection

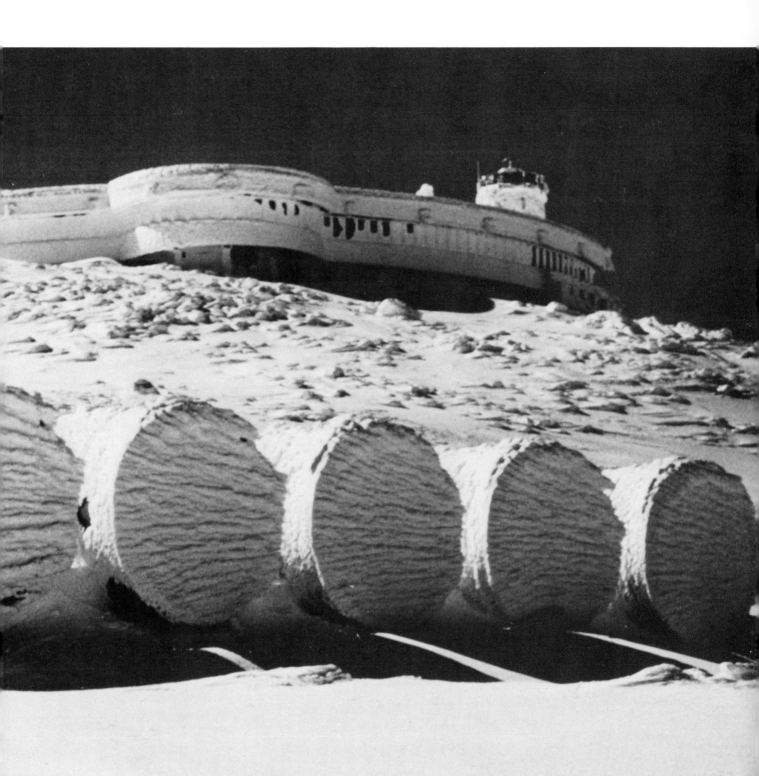

The new Summit House was semi-circular in design. This is a view of the summit as it appears at the present time. Mount Washington Observatory Staff Photo

First Day Cover issued on the anniversary of the 231-miles-per-hour wind recorded on Mount Washington in 1934.

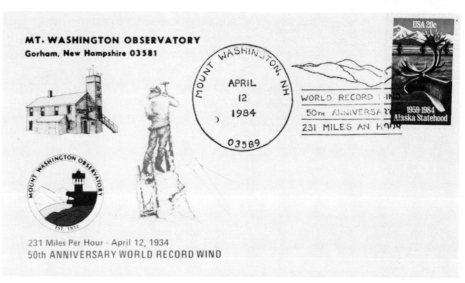

MT. WASHINGTON OBSERVATORY
Gorham, New Hampshire 03581

MOUNT WASHINGTON, NH
APRIL 12 1984
03589

WORLD RECORD WIND
50TH ANNIVERSARY
231 MILES AN HOUR

USA 20c
1959-1984 Alaska Statehood

MOUNT WASHINGTON OBSERVATORY
EST. 1932

231 Miles Per Hour · April 12, 1934
50th ANNIVERSARY WORLD RECORD WIND

The observatory tower on the summit of Mount Washington is shown in a stereo view by B. W. Kilburn. From the author's collection

Camden Cottage, on the right, was used by Dartmouth faculty and students for weather observations during the 1926 Christmas vacation. Photo by Winston Pote; courtesy of Mount Washington Observatory Collection

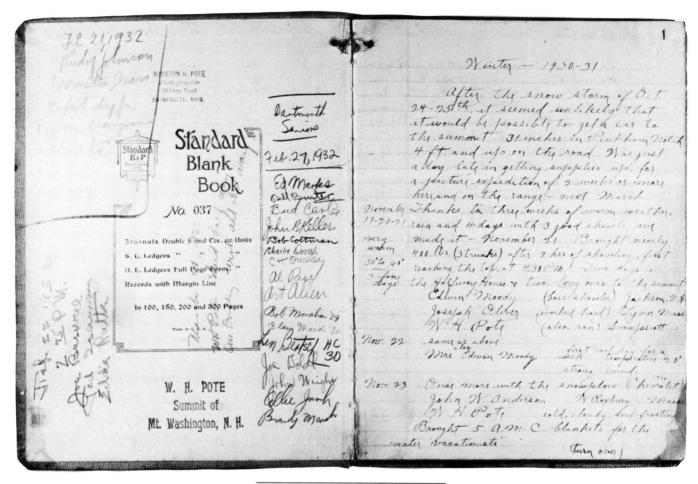

Winston Pote's sign-in book for the Summit House during the winter of 1931. Courtesy of Mount Washington Observatory Collection

near the Summit House for the use of the United States Coast and Geodetic Survey. In August 1892 a giant searchlight was mounted on the tower to determine the distances from which it would be possible to signal from elevated points. The operation could communicate with the observation tower ninety miles away in Portland, Maine, by using Morse code. The tower was popular with visitors, but it was torn down in 1902 because it was considered unsafe.

Many scientists conducted individual studies at the summit after the old weather station was abandoned in 1892. Robert Monahan with a small group of Dartmouth instructors and students, backpacked numerous instruments to the summit during the 1926 Christmas vacation. They made observations of the wind and weather during the brief period that they occupied the Camden Cottage. In the winter of 1931, Winston Pote, Joseph Oliver, and a little dog, Rex, spent two months in the Camden Cottage.

Pote, an expert photographer and mountain climber, went to the summit to photograph Mount Washington during the period when winter changes into spring.

The International Polar Year Commission emphasized the importance of mountain stations in studying upper air conditions in 1923-33. The occupation of Mountain Washington for full-time weather observations became a study in cooperation. The owners of the Mount Washington Summit Road made the stage office available to serve as an observatory. The AMC provided cots, bedding, and kitchen utensils. The New Hampshire Academy of Science donated four hundred dollars in cash, and the personnel were all volunteers. Alexander McKenzie, Robert Monahan, and Salvatore Pagliuca were joined by Nanook, an Eskimo sled dog. Joe Dodge kept in touch with them from the Pinkham Notch Camp through his shortwave radio.

The stage office was weatherproofed and equipped

The staff of the observatory in 1932-33. Left to right: Alexander McKenzie, Robert Monahan, Joseph Dodge, and Salvatore Pagliuca. Photo by Harold Orne; courtesy of Mount Washington Observatory Collection

with meteorological equipment during late September and early October. The building was completely insulated, new floors laid, storm windows added, and wiring installed. A soft coal-burning stove was set up so that the stove pipe passed through the ceiling into the bunkroom, where it elbowed into the chimney.

Winter observations produced a mass of information including some of the geological and chemical nature of snow sediment and the origins of atmospheric dust. On April 12, 1933, the observers experienced a blue snow-storm. Footprints appeared blue, a pail of melting snow filled with blue water, and the windows of the observatory looked like blue-stained glass. It was proposed that the blue color was caused by fine volcanic dust that had been swept through the stratosphere and deposited through the conditions created in a snowstorm.

The observatory, with occasional summer moves to the Camden Cottage, occupied the stage office for five years. On April 12, 1934, the greatest windspeed ever recorded spun the anemometer at the rate of 231 miles per hour. Winds of this speed would flatten the average wood frame building, but the rugged buildings on Mount Washington are chained or bolted to rocks and, on that day in 1934, every structure was buttressed with ice. In 1937 Henry Teague built a new observatory framed with nine-by-ten-inch railroad beams anchored with long bolts that extended into the rocks or concrete. The United States Weather Bureau supported the observatory from 1936 to 1951, furnishing about half the personnel and most of the weather equipment. Since 1951 the Weather Service, as well as other government agencies and private businesses, have contracted with the observatory to provide observational and research services.

In 1949 policies were changed to permit colleges, universities, and other institutions to participate in the research program. The Mount Washington Observatory

became an outstanding meteorological research station
and performed landmark work in the field of icing and
cloud research. The new observatory in the Sherman
Adams Summit Building has room for twelve people but
is usually staffed with two to five members who operate
the facility on a year-round basis. Their quarters include
a darkroom, a large room for weather instruments, and a
laboratory. There is an electronics repair and radio room
and additional space for scientific studies. The observatory's collection of White Mountain literature, prints,
photographs, and other artifacts is also housed on
the premises.

The observatory takes eight weather readings daily
and transmits the information to the United States
Weather Bureau at Portland, Maine. The Brooks Memorial
Tower provides a safe and convenient area for taking
weather observations and conducting experiments. The
top of the tower is at an elevation of 6,309 feet and has a
360 degree unobstructed view. The Observatory Museum
on the lower level provides visitors with dioramas, photo
exhibits, natural history displays, and memorabilia that
explain the history of the mountain. The observatory is a
non-profit organization with over three hundred members.

Skiing as a recreational activity began to undergo
drastic changes. In the 1930s there were not many skiers
and those who did participate in the sport tended to be

Three skiers enjoyed an outing on the trails of Wildcat Mountain. Photograph by Dick Smith; courtesy of Wildcat Mountain

rugged individualists. Ski trails were few and any uphill device was a welcome improvement. This group asked for little but the chance to ski and were content with a hot dog or sandwich for lunch. At night they lodged at one of the many fifty-cent-per-bed accommodations such as Ma Wilson's unheated establishment at Gorham. However, after World War II the sport exploded with significant changes in equipment and apparel. The social aspect became increasingly important, and skiers wanted the appropriate environment in which to exhibit their expensive clothing. They wanted large, attractive base buildings with picture windows facing the slopes, sundecks, good food served quickly, clean restrooms, and attractive shops.

The new generation of skiers wanted rapid surface lifts and, above all, they did not want to wait in line for their rides.

In 1938-39, Cannon was recognized as one of a few major ski areas. At that time, its three principal trails were unsurpassed and a maintenance crew kept them in shape, a real innovation in those days. The Tramway, although its limited capacity caused waiting lines from the very beginning, did provide a wonderful ride up the mountain. The trail system was improved somewhat after the war, but nothing was done then to upgrade the facilities. The mountain could not handle enough skiers to support more than a handful of inns, waiting lines became long,

Skiers lined up to use the Mount Cranmore skimobile during the winter of 1939-40. Photograph by Bray; courtesy of Mount Cranmore

and old customers began to look for new facilities. The base building had originally been a prefab salt box. It had evolved into a building with a ski shop, flush toilets, a small lounge, and a basic cafeteria. Skiers were demanding amenities such as daycare for their children and luxuries such as sundecks. Cranmore, which was privately owned, made adjustments to encourage weekday skiers, but the developments in New Hampshire had not kept pace with the times. This was particularly true of the small areas, which were not attracting the capital with which to upgrade their facilities. In 1961 the New Hampshire Planning and Development Commission submitted a report to the legislature which recommended that steps be taken

immediately to upgrade the ski facilities and initiate long-range planning for future development.

The commission recommended that Cannon add a high-capacity lift paralleling the Tram, initiate a trail modernization program, develop the Snow Bowl, purchase equipment to facilitate trail construction and maintenance, buy snowmaking equipment for lower Cannon, and replace rope tows with T-Bars. Wildcat needed trail improvements, new trails, an extension of the gondola (a system of suspended cars), a new base building, and a summit restaurant. Waterville Valley had no plans for immediate expansion.

Professional model Blanche Rybizka doing her best to promote skiing at Mount Cranmore during the winter of 1940-41. Photograph by Bray; courtesy of Mount Cranmore

A rope tow being used by skiers during the 1939-40 season. Photograph by Bray; courtesy of Mount Cranmore

Lines of skiers waiting to use the lift at Mount Cranmore during the 1939-40 season. Photograph by Bray; courtesy of Mount Cranmore

Facilities for skiers at Mount Cranmore in the early 1940s. Courtesy of Mount Cranmore

Harvey D. Gibson, a native of North Conway and the first owner of Mount Cranmore, is shown reading a Saturday Evening Post *article, "New Hampshire—the Poor Man's Snow Heaven." Photograph by Bray; courtesy of Mount Cranmore*

*This 1969 photograph is entitled
"Plowing Out the T-Bar." Courtesy of
Wildcat Mountain*

*Snowmaking equipment extends the ski
season and provides better skiing conditions when the weatherman doesn't
cooperate. Courtesy of Wildcat
Mountain*

New ski trails were built to accommodate the increasing number of skiers who came to the White Mountain ski resorts. Photograph by Dick Smith; courtesy of Wildcat Mountain

The Kancamagus Highway is a scenic east-west road connecting Conway with Lincoln, New Hampshire. Courtesy of University of New Hampshire Media Services

When Olympic skier Tom Corcoran came to Waterville Valley in 1965, the town comprised a single hotel, a group of cottages, and a small band of regular visitors. The valley had no zoning, no building codes, and no public utilities. The guests at Waterville Inn had always sought to keep the town unchanged and they convinced the United States Congress to put all but five hundred acres of the valley's forty-three thousand acres into the White Mountain National Forest. In 1937 the Civilian Conservation Corps put the first ski trail on Mount Tecumseh, and the first rope tow was installed on a slope behind the Inn in 1941.

In 1966 Corcoran laid out a network of twenty-one trails on Mount Tecumseh, installed four chairlifts, one T-bar, and thirty acres of snowmaking. During its opening season, in 1966-67, Waterville Valley attracted seventy-six thousand visitors, more than any other ski resort in New Hampshire. The Waterville Inn burned to the ground during that first winter season. It was replaced the following summer with two new inns and a restaurant. A resort condominium complex was started in 1969. Over the next ten years the town of Waterville Valley added a municipal water system, a sewer system with waste treatment plant, a public building with police and fire facilities, and an elementary school. Eventually, Waterville Valley Ski Resort grew to thirty-seven ski runs on two mountains, ten ski

lifts, and sixty instructors in its ski schools. There were five inns, three restaurants, the White Mountain Conference Center, five hundred condominium units, sixty-five single-family homes, eighteen clay tennis courts, a nine-hole golf course, a pond for swimming and boating, and a summer day camp for children.

The Mount Tecumseh ski area was the site of the first professional freestyle event ever held, and has hosted World Cup ski races, attracting the best international ski racers.

The Loon Mountain resort was developed by Sherman Adams, who had been a resident of the White Mountain logging town of Lincoln for nearly thirty years. Adams resigned from the Eisenhower administration in 1958, returned to New Hampshire, and six years later began making plans for a ski resort. The Kancamagus Highway, linking Lincoln and Conway, was completed in 1961, and Interstate 93 was working its way north to Lincoln. Loon Mountain was large enough to accommodate five thousand skiers and was only three miles from the path of the interstate.

Ninety acres of Loon Mountain were cleared for ten trails. A gondola and two chair lifts were ready to operate by Christmas of 1967, and the mountain attracted 30,000 skiers during its first year of operation. Eventually there were twenty-eight trails for skiers of all levels of skill.

A view of Dixville Notch from Table Rock. Photograph by C. P. Hibbard; courtesy of Stephen P. Barba

Snowmaking was added to cover 75 percent of the area, and six lifts brought 223,000 skiers to Loon Mountain during the 1981-1982 season.

The Balsams is a resort in Dixville Notch that began in 1873 as a three-story summer hotel that held fifty guests. By 1916 Henry Hale had turned the Balsams into a major grand resort with accommodations for four hundred guests. Much of the land on this fifteen-thousand-acre estate was purchased from the Brown Paper Company to protect the magnificent view. Neil Tillotson, the successful founder of the Tillotson Rubber Company, acquired the property in a federal foreclosure auction in 1954. He moved his rubber company operations to the Balsams and built the Wilderness Ski Area to enable him to operate the resort year-round. Winter business began to improve steadily and by 1970, the winter season attracted more guests than that summer. Today the Balsams operate at near capacity in both seasons, and the Wilderness Ski Area has become the thirteenth largest in the state. Dixville Notch, the community that votes first in the nation for all national primaries and general elections, has become an independent and productive community.

The aerial tramway at Cannon Mountain in Franconia Notch was replaced with a $4.7 million facility which reaches the summit of the forty-two-hundred-foot mountain in six minutes. The first aerial tramway in North America had a capacity of twenty-seven passengers. The new installation has a capacity of eighty passengers, and the ride offers spectacular views of Maine, Vermont, Canada, and even the Adirondacks of New York. Expanded facilities at Attitash in Bartlett, Mount Cranmore in North Conway, and Wildcat in Jackson have made New

Hampshire's White Mountains one of the most popular ski areas in the world.

Forty years after the dramatic campaign to save Franconia Notch, the rapid expansion of the interstate highway system again threatened the notch and the Old Man of the Mountains. Several studies were done to locate a highway between Plymouth and Franconia, but routes alternate to one through the notch proved unacceptable. Studies indicated that a large percentage of the traffic was to destinations in the notch, and a route that bypassed the area would not meet this need. Many businessmen supported the plan for modern highways, but others were opposed to committing the land area that would be required by an interstate. There was concern that blasting might damage the Old Man.

Conservationists were aided by the Yarborough Amendment to the Federal Highway Act which provided the road could be built in such an area only if there was no feasible alternative and that "all possible planning to minimize harm" must be done before such land can be used for highway purposes. Publicity about the controversy led to the altering of interchanges to use less land and preservation of scenic areas in the notch. Construction of the 11.6-mile Franconia Notch Parkway, completed in the fall of 1987, included the Gilman Visitors Center at the Flume. The new roadway had four lanes from Exit 32 at North Woodstock to the Whitehouse Bridge on the southern border of Franconia State Park. Throughout the park, there are two lanes divided by a "rumble strip" of flat granite blocks, a northbound climbing lane, and scenic parking areas at the Flume, the Basin, Lafayette Place, Boise Rock, Profile Lake, and Old Man, and Cannon Mountain.

THE BALSAMS OF DIXVILLE NOTCH

Eastman's *White Mountain Guide,* published in July 1866, pointed out that the Dixville hills were in the extreme northern portion of New Hampshire and it was seldom that tourists strayed so far from the regular routes. However, the completion of the Grand Trunk Railway meant that one could leave Boston at seven o'clock in the morning and sleep that night within ten miles of the notch. Guests at the Alpine House in Gorham could take the eleven o'clock train and ride thirty-six miles to North Strafford. A wagon-stage would meet the train at North Strafford and convey all passengers to Colebrook. Travelers were advised to pass the night at the Monadnoc House or the Parsons House as there were no public accommodations near Dixville Notch. Guests could leave the hotel at seven the next morning and devote the whole day to an excursion through the notch.

The Dix House was built in the notch on land formerly owned by ex-governor Dix of New York. It was opened to the traveling public on July 4, 1875, with many distinguished guests, including the ex-governor himself. According to *Farrar's Illustrated Guide to the Androscoggin Lakes,* "Lovers of the gun and rod found excellent sports in the vicinity, while pleasure-seekers and tourists were delighted with the scenery by which the house was surrounded. Raspberries grew in luxurious profusion near the hotel, and guests could always procure plenty of this delicious fruit." At that time the Dix House had about fifty rooms, a good livery stable, and accommodations were two dollars per day. It was managed by George Parsons.

The number of tourists increased, and the hotel was enlarged to accommodate 250 guests. Rooms were advertised as having steam heat, hardwood floors, electric lights, private baths, roomy closets, and tasteful furnishings. A handsome new dining hall was placed at the east end, and a new music room, for entertainment and dancing, was added on the west end. The kitchen was supplied by several farms operated by the company and trout, fresh from the waters of Lake Gloriette, was served daily for breakfast. A spring, high on the mountain, supplied the hotel with pure, sparkling water for all purposes. Camp Millsfield, ten miles to the southeast, was available to guests who preferred to "rough it" for a few hours, a few days or for their entire vacation.

Recreational facilities included a bowling green, tennis courts, trap shooting, and an eighteen-hole golf course designed by Donald J. Ross. The golf course and clubhouse were opened for the season of 1915. Lake Gloriette, sixty yards from the hotel, contained thousands of square-tailed trout. Canoeing and swimming were also enjoyed by the guests.

The Balsams Winter Inn was constructed to meet the demands of those who wished to remain at the notch when the main hotel was closed. It could sleep forty guests and was an excellent base for hunters and winter sports enthusiasts. Sleighing, coasting, snowshoeing, and skiing attracted visitors to Dixville Notch during the winter season.

Henry Hale, a successful inventor, purchased the Balsams because he was free from hay fever in the mountains. He spent a fortune in Dixville Notch, building an immense structure with eight hundred rooms. The building was four stories high, with steel frame, walls and partitions of tile and concrete, and fireproof floors. Nearly all of the rooms had a view of Lake Gloriette and the notch. The resort was very successful, but Hale made heavy investments in German bonds and was wiped out during the First World War.

Frank Doudera, a successful New York interior decorator, came to the Balsams during that period. So tastefully did the Doudera Decorating Company refurbish the eight hundred rooms, that the Balsams and Dixville Notch once again joined the ranks of such select establishments as Sugar Hill, the Mountain View House, Peckett's, and Bretton Woods.

Many of the large hotels in the White Mountains became victims of changing vacation patterns during the 1940s and 1950s. Neil Tillotson acquired the Balsams property in a federal foreclosure auction and developed plans to make it a year-round resort. He opened the Wilderness ski area and, eventually, more guests came in the winter than in the summer. In addition to skiing, they could snowmobile on a 110-mile network of trails, ice skate on a lighted rink, and go tobogganing, sledding, or snowshoeing.

The Balsams still operates in the style of New Hampshire's grand hotels and is the only survivor of that colorful period in the state's history. Charming atmosphere, elegant surroundings, excellent service, and superb cuisine have enabled the Balsams to survive while other large summer hotels have been victims of developers or condominium conversion.

Colby Street in Colebrook, New Hampshire, circa 1908. Courtesy of Stephen P. Barba

A post card view showing how the Dix House was expanded to become the Balsams. Courtesy of Stephen P. Barba

The original Dix House in Dixville Notch from a stereograph by B. W. Kilburn. Courtesy of Stephen P. Barba

"The Balsams" Dixville N.H.

The clubhouse at the Balsams Country Club. Courtesy of Stephen P. Barba

Dixville Notch provides a beautiful setting for the Balsams Country Club and golf course. Courtesy of Stephen P. Barba

Lake Gloriette and the Balsams resort hotel in Dixville Notch. Courtesy of Stephen P. Barba

The Balsams Winter Inn, Dixville Notch, N. H.

The Balsams Winter Inn was built to house winter sports enthusiasts and extend the tourist season. Courtesy of Stephen P. Barba

A steel-frame addition was added to the original structure. The Hampshire House advertised all the latest features to provide safety and comfort for the guests. Courtesy of Stephen P. Barba

The last of New Hampshire's grand resort hotels as it appeared when the large addition was completed. Courtesy of Stephen P. Barba

EPILOG

In 1901 Frank W. Rollins convened a meeting in Concord to discuss ways to save the White Mountains. At that time there were an estimated thirty-one hundred loggers in the state working for 680 different lumber companies. Five decades of logging and careless fires had reduced the region to a wasteland. It soon became obvious that a federal forest reserve act was the only way to save New Hampshire's mountains, and a public/private partnership was needed to achieve that goal.

The Society for the Protection of New Hampshire Forests and its supporters waged a dogged ten-year campaign which resulted in congressional approval of legislation that provided funds for the creation of the White Mountain National Forest, New England's largest tract of public land. The thousands of visitors who annually enjoy the spectacular mountain scenery are the beneficiaries of the struggle to preserve the eastern forests.

On August 3, 1923, guests playing tennis at the Profile House in Franconia Notch noticed smoke rising from the building. By the time firefighters could reach the attic, the place was an inferno. The flames spread quickly, but there was no panic. Staff members helped the guests get out of the hotel with their baggage. Not a single person was hurt nor a piece of baggage lost. Karl Abbott, owner of the Profile House, read about the fire while riding in a New York taxicab. He rushed to the notch and found his little mountain community a pile of smoldering ashes. Karl sat on a cracker box with an emergency telephone and called resort hotels all over New England. By evening he had all the guests in rooms, every member of the staff in a new job, and had transportation to get them all to their destinations.

Abbott began immediately making plans for a new hotel. His father, one of the early White Mountain hotel

Hannes Schneider teaching a ski school class in 1941. Photograph by Dick Smith; courtesy of Mount Cranmore

Harvey D. Gibson riding the Mount Cranmore skimobile during the winter of 1940-41. Gibson helped to finance the invention of the skimobile. Photograph by Bray; courtesy of Mount Cranmore

owners, persuaded him that the site should become part of a state park. He sold his holdings for $400,000, half of which came from the state of New Hampshire. The other half was raised by the Society for the Protection of New Hampshire Forests. The Franconia Notch Forest Reservation and Memorial Park was dedicated in 1928. The property is now in the hands of the state and will be shared with everyone who wants to visit.

The White Mountain National Forest now contains approximately 725,000 acres of land. This includes one thousand miles of trails for hikers, seven hundred miles of trout streams for fishermen and seventy-six ponds and lakes which are used by nearly five million vacationers each year. The new federal program eventually led to purchases of land in forty-eight national forests across the nation. The spark ignited in the White Mountains led to a national movement for the conservation of forest resources.

Hannes Schneider opened the first ski school in Austria in 1907. Schneider came to America in 1938, when the Nazi government came to power. He joined Harvey Dow Gibson to establish one of the first ski resorts in America. "The father of modern skiing" popularized the crouch position known as the Arleberg technique. With the support of banker Harvey Gibson, Schneider commissioned inventor George Morton to build Mount Cranmore's skimobile, the oldest ski lift in operation today. Mount Cranmore now has a new lodge, seven ski lifts, and a 100 percent snowmaking system.

Wildcat Mountain caters to the more advanced skier and features the first and oldest gondola still operating in New England. The views are spectacular! Nothing in the East can equal what can be seen from the top of Wildcat Mountain, which faces Mount Washington and Tuckerman's Ravine. Few slopes get more snow than Wildcat, and the north-facing slopes provide late spring skiing. There are no massive real estate developments, only great skiing.

Attitash consistantly offers some of the finest skiing in the eastern United States and had recently spent $3.5 million to add to the facilities. The Balsams/Wilderness stands alone as one of the nation's most magnificent resort settings. The fifteen-thousand-acre resort estate is surrounded by the towering walls of Dixville Notch and was called by *SKI Magazine* "one of the world's twelve poshest ski hotels." Black Mountain is in Jackson, a tiny country town that is entered through a covered bridge. Bretton Woods has twenty-one trails ranging from beginning to expert and has 90 percent snowmaking coverage. Cannon boasts the aerial tramway and is one of the most demanding ski developments in the East. In addition to great skiing, Loon Mountain has the J. E. Henry railroad, which transports skiers between the base station and the lodge. Loon sells a limited number of lift tickets, but only three or four other New England ski areas accommodated more people last winter. Waterville Valley guarantees that if a beginner spends five days in its ski school, a new skier will be born. It also offers a complete cross-country ski vacation with all the benefits of a resort area.

Winter in the White Mountains is filled with sports and snow, with family fun, unparalleled scenery and modern outdoor recreational facilities. Winter comes alive in New Hampshire. In the White Mountains it is very special.

*Profile Mountain at Franconia Notch.
Courtesy of University of New Hampshire Media Services*

Rock climbers at Franconia Notch. Photograph by Ron Bergeron

The Swift River runs along the Kancamagus Highway. Courtesy of University of New Hampshire Media Services

The gondolas at Wildcat Mountain Ski Resort. Photograph by Ron Bergeron

NCAA cross country ski races at Jackson, New Hampshire. Photograph by John Bardwell

The view of Mount Washington from the Wildcat Mountain ski trails. Photograph by Ron Bergeron

The beautiful covered bridge at Jackson, New Hamsphire. Photograph by John Bardwell

The Balsams-Wilderness Ski Area at Dixville Notch. Photograph by Ron Bergeron

BIBLIOGRAPHY

Books

Abbott, Karl P. *Open for the Season*. Garden City, New York: Doubleday & Company, Inc., 1950.

American Alps, Other Summer Haunts and Winter Retreats. Bethlehem, New Hampshire: The White Mountain Echo, 1892.

Anderson, Leon. *World's First Cog Railway*. Concord, New Hampshire: The Village Press, Inc., 1978.

Atkinson, Brooks, and W. Kent Olson. *At Home in the Wild*. Boston: Little Brown and Company, 1978.

Ball, Dr. B. L. *Three Days on the White Mountains, being the Perilous Adventure of Dr. B. L. Ball on Mount Washington, during October 25, 26, and 27, 1885, Written by Himself—A Thrilling Narrative*. Boston: Nathaniel Noyes, 1856.

Bartlett, John Henry. *A Synoptic History of the Granite State*. New York: M. A. Donohue & Company, 1939.

Beals, Charles Edward, Jr. *Passaconaway in the White Mountains*. Boston: Richard D. Badger, 1916.

Belcher, C. Francis. *Logging Railroads of the White Mountains*, Boston: Appalachian Mount Club, 1980.

Belknap, Jeremy. *The History of New Hampshire*. 2 vols. New York and London: Johnson reprint, 1970. Originally 1784, 1791, and 1792 as three volumes.

Bisbee, Ernest E. *The White Mountain Scrapbook of Stories and Legends of the Crystal Hills of the White Mountains of New Hampshire*. Lancaster, New Hampshire: The Bisbee Press, 1938.

Bruns, Paul E. *A New Hampshire Everlasting and Unfallen*. Concord, New Hampshire: The Society for the Protection of New Hampshire Forests, 1969.

Burt, F. Allen. *The Story of Mount Washington*. Hanover: Dartmouth Publications, 1960.

Carpenter, Frank O. *Guide Book to the Franconia Notch and the Pemigewasset Valley*. Boston: Alexander Moore, 1898.

Crawford, Lucy. *The History of the White Mountains from the First Settlement of Upper Coos and Pequaket*. Portland, Maine: Hoyt, Fogg & Dunham, 1883.

Cross, George N. *Dolly Copp and the Pioneers of the Glen*. Baltimore: Day, 1927.

Drake, Samuel. *The Heart of the Mountains*. New York: Harper & Brothers, 1882.

Early, Eleanor. *Behold the White Mountains*. Boston: Little, Brown and Company, 1935.

Ericson, Jonathon E., and Barbara A. Purdy, eds. *Prehistoric and Lithic Production*. Cambridge: Cambridge University Press, 1984.

Foss, Emma M. *Stage Coach Days in Plymouth*. Plymouth: Daughters of the American Revolution, 1921.

Gauch, Patricia Lee. *The Impossible Major Rogers*. New York: G. P. Putnam's Sons, 1977.

Gilmore, Robert C. *New Hampshire Literature: A Sampler*. Hanover: the University Press of New England, 1981.

Gramly, Richard M. *The Adkins Site: A Paleo-Indian Habitation and Associated Stone Structure*. Buffalo, New York: The Persimmon Press, 1988.

Greenleaf, C. H., *History, Old Man of the Mountain, the Flume, 1857-1931*. Boston: F. B. Moulton & Company, 1923.

Griffin, Nancy. *The Remarkable Stanley Brothers and Their Amazing Cars*. Portland, Maine: Guy Gannett Publishing Company, 1987.

Hanrahan, E. J., ed. *Bent's Bibliography of the White Mountains*. Somersworth: New Hampshire Publishing Company, 1971.

Harrington, Karl Pomeroy. *Walks and Climbs in the White Mountains*. New Haven: Yale University Press, 1926.

Hawthorne, Nathaniel. *Mosses From An Old Manse*. Boston: Ticknor and Fields, 1854.

Hawthorne, Nathaniel. *The Story of the Great Stone Face*. Littleton, New Hampshire: Courier Print Company, 1955.

Hawthorne, Nathaniel. *Tales of the White Hills and Sketches*. New York: Houghton, Mifflin & Company, 1889.

Hawthorne, Nathaniel. *Twice Told Tales*. Boston: Tichnor, Reed and Fields, 1851.

Hinton, John Howard. *History and Topography of the United States of America*. London, 1831.

Hosmer, James Kendall, ed. *Winthrop's Journal: History of New England, 1630-1649*. New York: Charles Scribner's Songs, 1908.

Jackson, Charles T. *Final Report of the Geology and Mineralogy of the State of New Hampshire*. Concord, 1844.

Jager, Ronald, and Grace Jager. *New Hampshire: An*

Illustrated History of the Granite State. Woodland Hills, California: Windsor Publications, Inc., 1983.

Kidder, Glen M. *Railway to the Moon.* Littleton, New Hampshire: Courier Printing Company, 1969.

Kilbourne, Frederick W. *Chronicles of the White Mountains.* New York: Houghton-Mifflin, 1916.

King, Thomas Starr. *The White Hills; Their Legends, Landscape, and Poetry.* New York: Hurd and Hougton, 1870.

Knickerson, Marion L., and John A. Downs. *Chocorua Peak House.* Center Conway, New Hampshire: Walker's Pond Press, 1977.

Oakes, William. *Scenery of the White Mountains.* Somersworth: The New Hampshire Publishing Company, 1970.

O'Kane, Walter Collins. *Trails and Summits of the White Mountains.* Boston: The Houghton Mifflin Company, 1925.

Olney, Susan Faxon, ed. *The White Mountains: Place and Perception.* Hanover: University Press of New England, 1980.

Packard, Winthrop. *Trails and Summits of the White Mountains.* Boston: Small, Maynard and Company, 1912.

Pillsbury, Hobart. *New Hampshire: Resources, Attractions, and Its People.* 5 vols. New York: The Lewis Historical Publishing Company, Inc., 1927.

Parley, Peter. *Book of Curiosities, Natural and Artificial.* Boston, 1832.

Poole, Ernest. *The Great White Hills of New Hampshire.* Garden City: Doubleday & Company, Inc., 1946.

Putnam, William Lowell. *Joe Dodge: One New Hampshire Institution.* Canaan, New Hampshire: Phoenix Publishing, 1986.

Randall, Peter. *Mount Washington: A Guide and Short History.* Hanover, New Hampshire: The University Press of New England, 1974.

Randall, Peter E. *Mount Washington: A Guide and Short History.* 2nd ed. Camden, Maine: Downeast Books, 1983.

Roberts, Kenneth. *Northwest Passage.* Garden City: Doubleday, Doran & Company, 1937.

Souvenir View Book of the White Mountains. Boston: Tichnor Brothers, Inc.

Spaulding, J. H. *Historical Relics of the White Mountains.* Boston: Hobart and Robbins, 1855.

Speare, Eva A. *Stories of New Hampshire.* Somersworth: The New Hampshire Publishing Company, 1975.

Sweetser, M. F. *The White Mountains: A Handbook for Travelers.* Boston: James R. Osgood and Company, 1876.

_____. *Views in the White Mountains.* Portland: Chisholm Brothers, 1879.

Vincent, Lee. *Instant Legends from the Rock Pile.* Somersworth: The New England History Press, 1975.

Vose, Arthur W. *The White Mountains: Heroes and Hamlets,* Barre, Massachusettes: Barre Publishers, 1968.

Waldron, Holman D. *With Pen and Camera Thro' the White Mountains.* Portland, Maine: Chisholm Brothers, 1905.

Ward, Julius H. *The White Mountains.* New York: D. Appleton & Company, 1890.

Welch, Sarah N. *A History of Franconia, New Hampshire.* Littleton: The Courier Printing Company, 1972.

Weygandt, Cornelius. *The White Hills.* New York: Henry Holt and Company, 1934.

Willey, Rev. Benjamin G. *Incidents in White Mountain History.* Boston: Nathaniel Noyes Publisher, 1856.

Willis, Nathaniel P. *American Scenery.* London, 1838-1839.

Yates, Elizabeth. *The Road Through Sandwich Notch.* Brattleboro, Vermont: The Stephen Greene Press, 1973.

Articles

Bahros, Anthony Nicholas. "History of the White Mountain National Forest." Master's thesis, University of New Hampshire, 1959.

Bofinger, Paul O. "Private Lands—Public Forest, The Story of the Weeks Act," *Forest Notes* (Summer 1986).

Elwell, Edward Henry. "The White Hills of New Hampshire." *Collections of the Maine Historical Society* 9 (1887).

Gramly, Dr. R. M. and S. L. Cox. "A Prehistoric Quarry-Workshop at Mt. Jasper, Berlin, New Hampshire." *Man in the Northeast* 11 (Spring 1976).

Gramly, Richard Michael. *Mount Jasper: Berlin, New Hampshire.* Berlin, New Hampshire: Smith & Town Printers, 1980.

Gramly, Richard Michael. "Raw Materials Source Areas and Curated Tool Assemblages." *American Antiquity,* 45 no. 4 (1980).

Johnson, John E. *The Boa Constrictor of the White Mountains or The Worst Trust in the World.* North Woodstock, New Hampshire, July 4, 1900.

New Hampshire Forestry and Recreation Commission. *A Report to the Legislature on the Present Status and Future Possibilities of Sports Activities in the Mount Washington, Pinkham Notch and Crawford Notch Areas of the White Mountains,* Concord, New Hampshire, 1955.

New Hampshire State Planning and Development Commission. *Winter Facilities Development: A Report to the 1961 Legislature.* Concord, New Hampshire, 1961.

Ober, Richard. "Notch Road Pushes Through." *Forest Notes* (Summer 1986).

Reid, Robert L. "Darby Field and the Christall Hill." *Mankind: Magazine of Popular History* 5, 1976-1977.

USDA Forest Service. *Draft Environmental Impact Statement, Land and Resources Management Plan, White Mountain National Forest.* Milwaukee, Wisconsin, 1984.

Views of the White Mountains. Portland, Maine: The Chisholm Brothers, 1907.

Videocassettes

"The White Mountains: A Cultural View." Durham: Department of Media Services, University of New Hampshire, 1980.

"White Mountains Lure." Concord: The Society for the Protection of New Hampshire Forests. Nd.

INDEX

John D. Bardwell, director of Media Services at the University of New Hampshire, is a 1955 graduate of University of New Hampshire. He served on the Maine Historic Preservation Commission for seven years and was chair for three years. He has produced films on archaeology, New Hampshire writers, the history of the White Mountains, the Piscataqua River basin, the history of America's submarines, and the history of the University of New Hampshire.

His publications include *The York Militia Company: 1642-1972* and *The Diary of the Portsmouth, Kittery and York Railroad*, and he was co-author of *Images of a University: A Photographic History of the University of New Hampshire*. He has recently completed the manuscript for a new book, *A History of the Country Club at York, Maine*.

Mr. Bardwell is a member of the Piscataqua Pioneers, the Society of Colonial Wars, and the Old York Historical Society. He is a proprietor of the Portsmouth Athenaeum. In 1979 he received the State of Maine Historic Preservation Award for his contributions to the state preservation program.

Ronald P. Bergeron, staff photographer with the Department of Media Services at the University of New Hampshire, is a 1972 graduate of the photography program at Franklin Institute of Technology in Boston. He has been a member of the staff at Media Services since that time.

Mr. Bergeron has provided photographs for many university publications, several textbooks, arts and crafts publications, slide-tape productions, and photographic exhibits. He produced the images for Mr. Bardwell's film on the University of New Hampshire and was co-author of the book *Images of a University*. He has worked extensively on the preservation of photographic images, lectures to local historical societies and civic organizations, and consults with them on conservation methods.

ST. JOHNSBURY

PASSUMPSIC

PASS. R.R.

PORT LAND AND OGDEN

LYNDONVILLE LUNENBURG

50.

SUMNR HOUSE DALTON

F. DODGE CHERRY MOUNT

BARNET

MT. INDOES

MONTPELIER

CONNECTICUT RIVER

VERMONT

CONNECTICUT RIVER

CONCORD &

N. LISBON

LISBON

OAK HILL HOUSE

UNION HOUSE

THAYER'S HOTEL

LITTLETON

WING ROAD

AMMONOOSUC RIVER

WHITE

WHITEFIELD HOUSE

WHITEFIELD

BROWN'S

OGDENSBURG R.R.

PORTLAND

JOHNS RIVER

JEFFE

FALLS

SINCLAIR HOUSE

BETHLEHEM STREET

MAPLE WOOD

BETHLEHEM STA.

CARROLL

TWIN MT STATION

TWIN MT HOUSE

FALLS

SUGAR HILL

FRANCONIA

ECHO LAKE

TAFT & GREENLEAF, PROFILE HOUSE

CRAWFORD HOUSE

WHITE MOUNTAIN HOUSE
FABYAN STATION

FABYAN HOUSE

MT. PLEASANT HOUSE

MT. WASHINGTON R.R.

CHERRY MOUNTAIN

OLD MAN MT.

NOTCH

WILLEY POND

WILLEY HOUSE

NOTCH

POOL
FLUME

WOODSVILLE

N. HAVERHILL

WELLS RIVER

NEWBURY

COOS

CAT

CANNON
4000

FLUME HOUSE

LAFAYETTE 5300

LINCOLN

WARREN   TOM   WILLARD

WEBSTER JACKSON
4000   4100

PORT

SMITH'S HOTEL
HAVERHILL

TUTTLE'S

NANCY BROOK

DR. BEMIS

E. HAVERHILL

WARREN

MOOSILAUK

N. WOODSTOCK

MERRIMAC RIVER

FOX

WOODSTOCK

A. CRAWFORD'S POND

SAWYER'S RIVER

S

BRADFORD

MOOSILAUK HOUSE

WENTWORTH

GRAFTON HOUSE

W. THORNTON

THORNTON

ORFORD

THEDFORD

LYME

POMPANOOSUC

SUMMIT

RUMNEY

W. RUMNEY

SANBORNS

CAMPTON VILLAGE

PROSPECT HOUSE

SENTER HOUSE

NORWICH

WHITE RIVER JUNCTION

WHITE RIVER JUNCTION

VT.

N

BAKERS

BLAIRS

ELM HOUSE

CAMPTON

PLYMOUTH

HANOVER

PEMIGEWASSET
HOUSE

WATER

ASHLAND

BRIDGE

MEREDITH

MOULTON HOUSE

CENTER HARBOR

LAKE
WINNIPISEOGEE

PAVILION
WOLFBOROUGH

OSSIPEE

WEST OSSIPEE

MC